THE OLD WEST'S
INFAMOUS
TRAIN ROBBERS
AND THEIR HISTORIC
HEISTS

W. C. JAMESON

TWODOT®

ESSEX, CONNECTICUT
HELENA, MONTANA

A · TWODOT® · BOOK
An imprint of Globe Pequot, the trade division of
The Rowman & Littlefield Publishing Group, Inc.
4501 Forbes Blvd., Ste. 200
Lanham, MD 20706
www.rowman.com

Distributed by NATIONAL BOOK NETWORK

British Library Cataloguing in Publication Information available

Library of Congress Cataloging-in-Publication Data Available
ISBN 978-1-4930-6662-9 (paperback)
ISBN 978-1-4930-6663-6 (ebook)

∞™ The paper used in this publication meets the minimum requirements of American National Standard for Information Sciences—Permanence of Paper for Printed Library Materials, ANSI/NISO Z39.48-1992.

CONTENTS

INTRODUCTION

America's train robbery era (1866–1924) represents a dramatic and tumultuous time in our nation's history. Nearly two hundred trains were stopped and robbed during this period, and millions of dollars' worth of gold and silver coins and ingots, currency, bank notes, and more were taken. The robbers were all daring men who placed their lives at risk stopping hundreds of tons of thundering engine, coal tender, and railroad cars to gain some amount of wealth. In many cases, passengers—men, and sometimes women—were killed.

The combination of trains and outlaws holds an automatic appeal and fascination for the American public. To this day, children as well as adults are easily attracted to and captivated by trains—the size, the sounds, the power manifested by these metal monsters. Outlaws capture our imaginations and appeal to some atavistic sense of freedom, of adventure, of daring. We have long been attracted to these rebellious souls, the rule breakers who thwart the wishes and motives of large corporate entities like railroads, banks, mining companies, and more.

During a survey in which more than three thousand people were asked to name at least three US presidents who served from 1865 through 1885, less than 3 percent could do so. When asked to name at least three famous outlaws who operated in that time period, most could identify Frank and Jesse James, Butch Cassidy, the Sundance Kid, the Doolin Gang, the Dalton Gang, and more. Incidentally, each of the named outlaws were noted for robbing trains.

The first railroad chartered in the United States was the Baltimore and Ohio Railroad in 1828. Because railroads were not common at the time, most goods and supplies, as well as money, bullion, and ore, were transported by wagons pulled by horses, mules, and/or oxen. Stagecoaches handled many shipments as well. As railroads expanded across the country, train travel was faster and more efficient for shipping goods and transporting people. In addition, the ever-expanding railroads provided jobs for a growing number of Americans. Dozens of towns today—small and large—had their beginnings as railroad stops. Railroads brought prosperity to places where heretofore there was none. They also brought a level of affluence to enterprising outlaws, men who realized that, robbing train cars, like banks, could be a source of income, albeit illegal.

Before long, the demand for shipment by rail was such that "express cars" were added to the array of train cars, which included the locomotive, the coal tender, livestock cars, and passenger coaches, rumbling down the tracks.

Railroad express cars were used to transport money, certificates, and other valuables, as well as mail (before specific mail cars were added). They were not designed to protect the contents from robbers because expectations of theft were low, at least originally. The first express cars were made of wood, the sides and doors easily pierced by bullets. In time, they were fitted with iron plates to repel gunfire, and were accompanied by one or more express "messengers," men whose job it was to protect the contents of the car. As express car security evolved, so did the train robbers. If firing bullets into the car didn't get the attention of the messenger, a few sticks of dynamite would.

The outlaws soon recognized another advantage—location. Robbers would board the train, gain access to the locomotive, and force the engineers to pull to a halt in a remote section of the countryside, far from law enforcement and pursuit. During the train robbery era, most outlaws got away with their heists, amounting to millions of dollars.

As train robberies increased, so did newspaper coverage of the events. As a result, a number of outlaws gained everlasting fame. With the increase in robberies came a gradual increase in security, however, and it was not unusual to find a single train accompanied by as many as a dozen law enforcement officers, some placed in the express cars, and others scattered throughout the passenger coaches. Further, law enforcement was expanding across the country, becoming established in many of the towns, large and small, that sprang up around train stations.

In addition to hiring local law enforcement, the railroads also contracted with private detectives and professional gunmen, often associated with the Pinkerton Detective Agency and the Wells, Fargo Express Company. Prevention and inhibition of train robbery, as well as the growing success record relative to pursuing, capturing, and sentencing the miscreants had reached a level of sophistication such that after 1924, train robbery had all but ceased.

To many, the train robbers of yore remain heroes of a sort. They were fearless men, adventurous souls undertaking an often dangerous task in order to reap some level of wealth. Further, the train robbers were men who thumbed their noses at authority, men who rebelled against the corporations, such as railroads and banks that had grown prosperous and powerful, oftentimes at the expense of the common man. Frank and Jesse James, who fought for the South during the Civil War, only robbed trains owned by northern railroad companies. Further, when passengers were robbed, Southerners were spared. Butch Cassidy held a particular dislike for large corporate entities because he saw that they often made their riches at the expense of honest and hardworking citizens.

A section titled "Some Railroad Terminology" is included at the end of this book, which offers definitions of many of the terms employed in the text.

With this publication, the reader is invited to enter the realm of some of America's most famous train robbers and their daring escapades, their historic heists. A few of these souls have become household names, lionized in films and books, and regarded as heroes by many. In addition, millions of dollars of train robbery loot that had been spirited away and cached somewhere is still missing to this day. More than a century after these events, these fascinating outlaws are still being researched and written about, and their train robbery loot is still being searched for.

Chronology

Date	Location	Perpetrator(s)
October 6, 1866	Seymour, Indiana	Reno Gang
May 22, 1868	Marshfield, Indiana	Reno Gang
July 10, 1868	Shields, Indiana	Reno Gang
July 21, 1873	Adair, Iowa	James Gang
January 31, 1874	Gads Hill, Missouri	James Gang
December 8, 1874	Muncie, Kansas	James Gang
September 18, 1877	Big Springs, Nebraska	Sam Bass
February 22, 1878	Allen, Texas	Sam Bass
March 18, 1878	Hutchins, Texas	Sam Bass
April 4, 1878	Eagle Ford, Texas	Sam Bass
April 10, 1879	Mesquite, Texas	Sam Bass
October 8, 1879	Glendale, Missouri	James Gang
July 15, 1881	Winston, Missouri	James Gang
September 7, 1881	Blue Cut, Missouri	James Gang
December 1, 1886	Bellevue, Texas	Rube Burrow
January 23, 1887	Gordon, Texas	Rube Burrow
May 18, 1887	McNeil, Texas	Unknown
June 4, 1887	Benbrook, Texas	Rube Burrow
June 18, 1887	Flatonia, Texas	Bill Whitley and Brack Cornett
September 30, 1887	Benbrook, Texas	Rube Burrow
December 9, 1887	Genoa, Arkansas	Rube Burrow
September 22, 1888	Harwood, Texas	Bill Whitley and Brack Cornett
December 15, 1888	Duck Hill, Mississippi	Rube Burrow
February 22, 1889	Pixley, California	Evans-Sontag Gang
September 11, 1899	Cochise Junction, Arizona	Burt Alvord
September 25, 1889	Buckatunna, Mississippi	Rube Burrow
January 20, 1890	Goshen, California	Evans-Sontag Gang
September 1, 1890	Century, Florida	Rube Burrow
February 6, 1891	Alila, California	Dalton Gang
May 9, 1891	Wharton, Indian Territory	Dalton Gang
September 3, 1891	Ceres, California	Evans-Sontag Gang
September 15, 1891	Leliatta, Indian Territory	Dalton Gang
June 1, 1892	Red Rock, Indian Territory	Dalton Gang
July 1, 1892	Kasota Junction, Minnesota	Evans-Sontag Gang

July 15, 1892	Adair, Indian Territory	Dalton Gang
August 3, 1892	Collis, California	Evans-Sontag Gang
October 13, 1892	Caney, Kansas	Doolin Gang
November 27, 1892	Malta, Montana	The Sundance Kid
May 19, 1893	Ponca Station, Indian Territory	Doolin Gang
June 9, 1893	Cimarron, Kansas	Doolin Gang
April 3, 1895	Dover, Indian Territory	Doolin Gang
May 14, 1897	Lozier Station, Texas	Black Jack Ketchum
June 2, 1899	Wilcox, Wyoming	The Wild Bunch
August 16, 1899	Folsom, New Mexico	Black Jack Ketchum
February 15, 1900	Fairbank, Arizona	Burt Alvord
July 3, 1901	Wagner, Montana	The Wild Bunch
December 30, 1914	Cline, Texas	Willis Newton
August 25, 1921	Bells, Texas	Newton Gang
September 6, 1921	Bloomberg, Texas	Newton Gang
November 8, 1921	Paxton, Illinois	Newton Gang
December 8, 1922	St. Joseph, Missouri	Newton Gang
June 11, 1924	Rondout, Illinois	Newton Gang

John Reno

1

The Reno Gang

THE RENO GANG IS GENERALLY CONSIDERED BY HISTORIANS AS HAVING committed the first peacetime train robbery in the United States on October 6, 1866. An investigation into this claim, however, reveals that a train holdup had occurred nine months earlier. On January 8, 1866, a New York, New Haven and Hartford Railroad train was stopped between New York and New Haven and robbed of an astonishing $700,000. The identities of the holdup men remain unknown, and details of the robbery are so few and contradictory, it has not been included in the book.

For the Reno brothers, outlaw ways were little more than family tradition. Their father, Wilkinson Reno, was rebuked when he tried to purchase some land from a neighbor. Irate at the refusal, the elder Reno responded by burning the residents out of Rockford, Indiana, a nearby village.

Eldest son Frank Reno had been arrested for robbing a post office, and John, the next oldest, was a suspect in at least one murder. Though charged, none of the brothers were ever brought to trial. Frank and John, along with younger brothers William and Simeon, organized a band of thieves who went about the region robbing banks and travelers, often leaving dead men in their wake.

A fifth brother, Clint—known as "Honest Clint"—never participated in any of the gang's illegal activities, departing markedly from the family tradition of outlawry.

Frank Reno

SEYMOUR, INDIANA

On October 6, 1866, an eastbound Ohio and Mississippi Railroad passenger train bound for Cincinnati, Ohio, became the victim of the Reno Gang. John and Simeon Reno, along with gang member Franklin Sparks, settled into a passenger coach as the train pulled away from the Seymour station. Several miles later as the train rolled through the countryside, the three men casually made their way out of the front of the car and paused on the platform of the Adams express car. Here, the two Reno brothers and Sparks forced their way into the car, surprising the messenger. Before he could sound the alarm, the messenger was knocked out from a blow to the head.

The robbers tried to open the safe but were stymied. They realized the only one who knew the combination was lying unconscious on the express car floor. Frustrated, the outlaws yanked the emergency cord, causing the train to slow down and pull to a stop. After opening the side door of the car, they shoved the safe out and onto the ground. This done, they moved about the express car searching for other riches, finally finding a leather pouch containing $10,000 to $12,000. (One account provided by the railroad company estimated $90,000 was taken in the heist.)

As the robbers pondered what to do with the safe, the engineer and fireman left the locomotive cab and were hastening back down the track to investigate the emergency. The Reno Gang forced the train crew at gunpoint back toward the engine, and returned their attention to the safe with a hammer and a pry bar. After flailing away at the heavy metal safe for another half-hour and having no success, the gang decided to be content with the cash and fled into the nearby woods.

Later when the train pulled in at the small town of North Vernon, Indiana, a report of the robbery was telegraphed back to Seymour where a posse was quickly formed. The pursuers gathered upon a handcar and hand-pumped their way down the track to the scene of the robbery. They found no sign of the robbers' departure, but they did recover the safe.

When questioned, the engineer and fireman related that they recognized the Reno brothers and Sparks. The men were subsequently indicted for the robbery in absentia, a first for this kind of crime in America.

In perhaps what may have been one of the earliest copycat crimes, two months later, two Seymour residents—Michael Collins and Walter Hammond—pulled off a nearly identical robbery of the same Adams express car at the same location where the Reno gang had stopped the Ohio and Mississippi Railroad train earlier. The robbers escaped with $8,000. When the Reno brothers learned of the holdup, they decided to track down the robbers and teach them a lesson about intruding on the territory of others.

Frank and Bill Reno caught up with Collins and Hammond before the copycats could spend any of the robbery loot. The Renos confiscated the money and kept it for themselves. Further, they turned their two victims over to Jackson County Sheriff John Scott, who charged them with the crime and jailed them. Frank and Bill even received a reward for capturing the robbers. The old adage "crime does not pay" did not apply to the Reno Gang.

Weeks following the capture of Collins and Hammond, John Reno ceded leadership of the gang to brother Frank. John then traveled to Gallatin, Missouri, where he robbed the Daviess County Treasury of $22,000. He was captured, tried, and sentenced to twenty-five years of hard labor in the Missouri State Penitentiary at Jefferson City.

As the new leader of the Reno Gang, Frank immediately turned his attention to robbing another train. He began planning the holdup of the Marshfield Express of the Jefferson, Missouri, and Indianapolis Railroad.

MARSHFIELD, INDIANA

The aptly named Marshfield is located in the Scott County lowlands about fifteen miles south of Seymour. Today it is a small, unincorporated community. It is so small, in fact, that it is not included in census counts.

In 1868, Marshfield was little more than a stop for the Jefferson, Missouri, and Indianapolis Railroad where the trains took on water and fuel. On the afternoon of May 22, the Reno Gang rode to Marshfield. It is suspected by most researchers that Frank Reno orchestrated the robbery with brothers William and Simeon, along with as many as ten more gang members, including Franklin Sparks. Sparks was instructed to mind the horses while the rest of the gang, divided into three groups, went about their assignments. Four of the outlaws, headed by Fril Clifton, climbed the telegraph poles and cut the wires.

Around 11 p.m., as the northbound train was taking on water, one of the two engineers on this run, David Hutchinson, was making his maintenance rounds. Carrying an oilcan, he inspected the wheels and other moving parts. As he was oiling the piston drive-rods, he was struck on the back of the head and, dazed, dropped to the ground.

Shortly after, two of the train's firemen were filling the boiler and reattaching the spout to the water tank, when they chanced upon the semiconscious Hutchinson. During subsequent questioning, the two men stated they had then seen four men materialize out of the darkness and begin to uncouple the express car from the rest of the train. Realizing they had been spotted, the robbers immediately surrounded the train employees and beat them. Another group of outlaws entered the cab and subdued the second engineer, knocking him unconscious and tossing him onto the right-of-way.

One of the outlaws then threw the throttle forward, causing the engine, tender, and express car to proceed down the track. As the train picked up speed, a conductor ran toward the engine firing a revolver. The outlaws fired back, but despite the exchange of several rounds no one was hit.

As the train raced away toward the north, three of the robbers made their way along a narrow walkway to the express car and broke into it through a side door. The messenger, F. G. Harkins, put up a brief resistance, but he was quickly subdued by the intruders. After inflicting a severe beating onto Harkins, they threw him out of the moving train into the swamp. The express company safes were attacked with crowbars, the contents removed, and stuffed into canvas bags. According to various reports, the robbers harvested between $40,000 and $96,000, with most researchers leaning toward the latter figure. Some reports state the loot was in the form of gold; others insist it was cash.

When the engine, tender, and express car had arrived one mile south of Seymour, the bandits pulled it to a stop near a point where horses had been tied earlier. After mounting up, the robbers rode away. A posse that arrived at the scene of the robbery several hours later had no luck in picking up their trail. All of the evidence suggested that it was the Reno Gang that had struck again.

The holdup of the Marshfield Express came to be referred to as "The Great Train Robbery," and has subsequently been proclaimed in song, story, and even a motion picture. It is believed by the majority of train robbery enthusiasts that subsequent robberies by the James Gang, the Doolin Gang, and the Dalton Gang were patterned after this Reno holdup.

SHIELDS, INDIANA

Frank Reno, along with brothers William and Simeon, decided to lay low for a while. Four other members of the gang agreed with him and fled to Canada. Six additional members of the gang, however, decided to rob another train. On the night of July 10, 1868, Franklin Sparks, John Moore, Henry Jerrell, Fril Clifton, Charlie Rosenberry, and Valliance Elliot boarded an express near Shields, six miles west of Seymour, where it had stopped long enough to take on water and fuel. Moore had somehow learned that the Adams Express was transporting $100,000 in gold coins.

Following a pattern established by Frank Reno, the outlaws stopped the train a short time after it departed Shields. Little did the gang know that a trap had been set for them. Earlier, the Pinkertons had created a phony announcement relating to the shipment of the large sum of money in hopes that the Reno Gang would attempt to take it. After forcing open the express car door, the outlaws were surprised by a barrage of bullets from several Pinkerton detectives who had stationed themselves in the car.

A brief exchange of gunfire followed the initial fusillade. Moore, Jerrell, Elliot, and Sparks were wounded, but all the outlaws managed to reach their awaiting horses and make their escape. A short time later, however, Elliot, Rosenberry, and Clifton were captured by the Pinkertons. While they were being transported back to Seymour to be charged, the group was overtaken by a band of vigilantes who seized the prisoners and hung them all on a sycamore tree by the side of the road.

Moore, Jerrell, and Sparks were tracked to Aetna, Illinois, where they were arrested, shackled, and placed on a train to be delivered to Seymour. Three miles from Seymour, the train was stopped by a party of an estimated two hundred men. Several boarded the train and took possession of the robbers. They carried them to a preselected spot along the road and hung them where their three companions had previously been lynched.

Simeon and William had fled to Indianapolis where they were identified and arrested. In order to evade the vigilantes at Seymour, the two were taken to New Albany, Indiana, and turned over to Sheriff Fullenlove.

Meanwhile, Frank Reno and Charlie Anderson were captured in Windsor, Ontario, and following a difficult extradition process, were returned to the United States heavily shackled and guarded by Pinkerton detectives. The two were eventually taken to New Albany where they were reunited with Simeon and William. News of the notorious Reno Gang incarceration in the town spread rapidly.

A loose-knit organization calling itself the "Southern Indiana Vigilance Committee" advanced on the jail and demanded the keys to the jail cells from Fullenlove. When he refused, they shot him. The Renos were taken from their cells and each one hung from a ceiling beam, thus effectively putting an end to the first train robbery gang in America.

A major question remains: What happened to the $96,000 in cash and/or gold taken from the Marshfield train robbery? According to legend, the entire amount was buried in a location treasure-hunters are searching for to this day.

During their escape following the Marshfield robbery, the gang fled into the swampy terrain so abundant in the area. They were guided by gang member John Moore, who had grown up in these environs, and had hunted and trapped throughout as a youth. According to legend, at a location approximately three miles from the robbery site and eight miles south of Seymour, Frank Reno called a halt. On his orders, the loot was removed from the horses and buried in the muddy ground.

There is no evidence that any of the gang members ever returned to this location to recover the $96,000. With the death of the Reno brothers, along with most of the other gang members, there is no one left with precise knowledge of the location of this cache. As far as anyone knows, it lies there still.

Jesse James

2

The James Gang

FOR MANY, THE NAME JESSE JAMES IS SYNONYMOUS WITH TRAIN ROBbery. Indeed, numerous accounts—books, articles, feature films, documentaries, and newspaper reports—have related the train holdups of America's most well-known gang of robbers.

In what is perhaps an apocryphal tale, when Jesse James was asked why he robbed trains, he reportedly replied, "Because that's where the money is." This is a true statement in fact, whether it came from James's lips or not. Wealth, in the form of cash, gold, silver, and notes, not in the hands of banks, corporations, and private citizens was often enroute from one place to another via train, packed away in an express car. Knowing this, Jesse James made these his targets. Jesse and his gang, which included his brother Frank, found that robbing trains and banks was easier and more lucrative than toiling away on the family farm. Jesse was in pursuit of money, to be sure, but was also in pursuit of adventure and, as it turned out, revenge.

Jesse Woodson James was born on September 5, 1847, to Robert and Zerelda James in Clay County, Missouri, and not far from the present-day town of Kearney. This region was settled primarily by migrants from the Upper South, most from Kentucky and Tennessee, and all with strong Southern sympathies. Jesse had a brother, Franklin (Frank), and a sister, Susan Lavenia. His father, Robert, was a farmer, a Baptist minister, and helped found William Jewell College of Liberty, Missouri. He farmed one hundred acres and possessed six slaves.

During the gold rush to California in the late 1840s, Robert traveled to the Golden State, allegedly to minister to those who were searching for wealth. He died there. Jesse was only three years old at the time. Jesse's mother, Zerelda, was remarried in 1852 to Benjamin Simms. The union did not last long, and by 1855 she had divorced Simms and married Dr. Reuben Samuel. Samuel moved onto the James family farm, and over the years the couple produced four additional children. Zerelda and Reuben also acquired an additional seven slaves and operated a relatively successful tobacco farm.

In early 1860, with the Civil War on the horizon, Missouri was regarded as a "border" state, exhibiting characteristics of both the North and South. Clay County was strongly Southern in culture and orientation and housed more slaves and slaveholders than any other portion of the state. By 1861 spates of violence erupted along the Kansas-Missouri border between pro- and anti-slavery militias.

A short time later, and following a series of skirmishes between conventional armies, guerrilla warfare descended on Missouri between Union forces ("jayhawkers") and secessionists ("bushwhackers"). The growing Union presence led to the enforcing of martial law, accompanied by raids on private homes and farms, arrests of civilians, summary executions, and the eviction of Confederate sympathizers from the state.

The James family was passionately pro-Confederate. Frank James enlisted in a local militia company and fought at the Battle of Wilson's Creek in August 1861. A short time later, he became ill and returned to the Clay County farm. In 1863, Frank was identified as a member of a guerilla unit that operated in and around Clay County. He became the target of a Union Army company that went in search of him. The company rode onto the James-Samuel farm looking for Frank and his associates.

During this time, Jesse remained on the farm and applied himself to the necessity of working in the fields, sometimes from dawn until dusk. He grew weary of such work, his mind and soul only barely tolerant of the tedium of this kind of life. Jesse longed for more—for adventure, to explore, to see what lay beyond the borders of Clay County. He was soon to get his chance.

Frank could not be found, but the Union soldiers came upon sixteen-year-old Jesse working in the fields. When he pleaded ignorant of his brother Frank's whereabouts, the soldiers whipped him viciously. Moments later, they turned their attention toward the kindly Dr. Samuel. When Samuel, described as a "quiet, passive man,"[1] likewise denied any knowledge of Frank's location, the troopers tortured the old man, repeatedly hanging and lowering him from the limb of a nearby tree.

Deprived of oxygen, and suffering the stress and trauma of torture, Dr. Samuel was never the same. He lived the remainder of his life as a semi-invalid. He spent the past eight years of his life in an institution and passed away in 1908.

The young and impressionable Jesse James was stunned by the brutal and unnecessary Union treatment of his beloved stepfather. He wanted to fight back, and the only way he knew how was to follow in his brother Frank's footsteps. Frank was now riding with a guerrilla unit led by William C. Quantrill, known and feared as Quantrill's Raiders. It is believed that Frank was part of Quantrill's unit that raided the abolitionist town of Lawrence, Kansas, slaughtering more than two hundred men and boys.

During the winter of 1863–1864, Frank returned to Clay County with a squad commanded by Fletch Taylor. The sixteen-year-old Jesse immediately joined his brother in Taylor's unit. During the summer of 1864, Jesse and Frank joined a bushwhacker group led by William "Bloody Bill" Anderson. During one skirmish, Jesse suffered a bullet wound to the chest.

As far as is known, Jesse's first encounter with a train occurred on September 27, 1864. According to the Clay County provost marshal, both Jesse and Frank participated in what has been called the Centralia Massacre. Quantrill's guerrillas stopped a train carrying twenty-four unarmed Union soldiers returning home from duty. The soldiers were taken off the train and executed. A number of the dead were scalped and mutilated by the guerrillas.

By the end of the war, Jesse was recovering from a second bullet wound, tended to by his first cousin, Zerelda Mimms. The two later married. As Jesse recuperated, Archie Clements, one of Quantrill's guerillas, assembled a gang of former soldiers, their intention being to continue to harass the authorities in power—the hated Yankees.

Most researchers are convinced that Clements and his toughs committed the first daylight armed bank robbery of the Clay County Savings and Loan Association in Liberty, Missouri, on February 13, 1866, a bank owned by former Union militia officers. It is also believed that Jesse and Frank James participated in the robbery, though no indisputable evidence for or against this proposition has ever surfaced.

The Clements Gang continued with their harassing activities and bank robberies over the next two years. During this time, the number of gang members decreased as a result of arrests, gunfights, and hangings. On May 23, 1867, the gang entered a bank in Richmond, Missouri, stole a small amount of money, and killed the town's mayor and two other citizens. Scholars are unclear as to the roles, if any, Jesse and Frank James had in these holdups, but most are convinced the two were involved. While neither of the brothers had a major part in any of them, it was clear they were experiencing some on-the-job training relative to bank robbery. In 1868 Jesse and Frank joined the outlaw Cole Younger in a Russellville, Kentucky, bank robbery.

Until the latter part of 1869, few were aware of, or had even heard the name, Jesse James in relation to the numerous bank robberies. On December 7 of that year, however, he and a small gang, which might have included Frank, robbed the Daviess County Savings and Loan Association in Gallatin, Missouri. During the robbery, Jesse shot and killed the cashier, John Sheets. It was later revealed that the young outlaw mistook Sheets for Samuel P. Cox, a militia officer who killed "Bloody Bill" Anderson during the Civil War.

The Gallatin robbery, according to Jesse James experts, represented the emergence of outlaw Frank James's brother into the public eye. Jesse was identified as "the most famous survivor of the former Confederate bushwhackers."[2] It was the first time the term "outlaw" was attached to his name.

Once again, the robbery netted relatively little money. An entrepreneurial outlaw, Jesse pondered other ways to harvest more money and at the same time wreak revenge on the hated Yankees.

As time passed, the notion of robbing a train remained firm in the mind of Jesse James. He and Frank joined up with Cole, John, Jim, and Bob Younger, along with Clell Miller and a handful of other former rebels. Eventually they came to be known as the James-Younger Gang, with Jesse as the most public face of the band. The group carried out a string of robberies from Iowa to Texas and from Kansas to West Virginia. They held up banks, stagecoaches, and even a fair in Kansas City. It was only a matter of time before the gang turned to train robbery.

ADAIR, IOWA

On July 21, 1873, the James-Younger Gang descended on a Chicago, Rock Island & Pacific Railroad passenger train near the small southwestern Iowa town of Adair. For years, a marker near this site referred to the event as the first train robbery in the United States, though this is far from the truth. It was, however, the first train robbery conducted by Jesse James and his gang.

The CRI&P train was eastbound and expected in Des Moines, sixty miles east of Adair, at 10:15 p.m. At three miles west of the Adair station, the gang loosened a rail, attached a rope to it, and employing their mounts, pulled it away from the tracks. To this day, the exact number of robbers, as well as their identities, have never been determined. Most historians are convinced, however, that Jesse and his brother Frank were involved.

On spotting the displaced rail up ahead, the engineer, John Rafferty, set the brakes and threw the engine's wheels into reverse, but given the momentum of the multi-ton speeding train, it was too late. When the train reached the damaged section of track, the engine, coal tender, express car, and baggage car careened off the tracks and into a nearby ditch. The front wheels of the first passenger car left the rails but the coach remained upright.

As the engine departed the track, Rafferty was slammed against one side of the cab and, it is believed, died instantly from a broken neck. Though injured, fireman Dennis Foley dragged Rafferty from the wreck. This done, the dedicated and responsible Foley crawled back to the engine and opened a relief valve on the boiler, thus preventing an explosion.

Following the derailment, the robbers, wearing Ku Klux Klan masks, rode toward the wreckage, firing their weapons into the cab. One bullet struck the thigh of the already dead engineer. The gang approached the Wells, Fargo express car. It was this car that transported money in the form of cash, coin, bullion, and more. It was reported that the CRI&P train was carrying three tons of gold and silver bullion stacked on the floor. The express car door was locked, so the robbers were forced to break it open.

Once inside, the robbers encountered the Wells, Fargo messenger, a man named Burgess. At gunpoint, they demanded of Burgess the location of the bullion. The frightened messenger pointed to the ingots that had been scattered across the floor of the car, most likely wondering how the robbers would be able to carry away all of that great weight. The gang ignored the ingots, which must have seemed odd to Burgess. It was later surmised that the gang members did not know the meaning of the term "bullion," believing it referred to bags of coins, which is what they were searching for.

Burgess was ordered to unlock the express company safe, from which was withdrawn approximately $1,700 in cash and a locked Wells, Fargo satchel, the contents of which were never revealed. (At least one account lists the amount stolen as $3,000.)

Weeks passed, and eventually a press release emanating from St. Louis stated that it was believed the robbers were from western Missouri and were the same ones who robbed the banks in Russellville, Kentucky; Gallatin, Missouri; and possibly St. Genevieve, Missouri. The press release listed the names of the presumed robbers: Jesse and Frank James, Cole Younger, Bill Sheppard, and a man named McCoy. Not long afterward, the Pinkerton National Detective Agency officially listed the James brothers as members of the gang, along with Frank Cole, Jim Younger, Clell Miller, Bob Moore, and a man named Comanche Tony.

Though Jesse and Frank James were listed in the St. Louis press release and Pinkerton reports as members of the Adair train robbery gang, some controversy exists regarding their actual participation. James scholars disagree among themselves over this issue.

The truth is, it has always been difficult to derive firm evidence relative to the activities of Jesse and Frank James. Author Richard Patterson states, "These two outlaws . . . often used assumed names and seldom remained in one place for any length of time. The few persons privy to their coming and going kept their mouths shut. In fact, whether Frank and Jesse actually took part in many of the robberies with which they have been credited may never be known."[3]

GADS HILL, MISSOURI

The first train robbery to take place in Missouri occurred at Gads Hill on January 31, 1874. It was the first of many, and during the next ten years Missouri was known far and wide as The Train Robbery State, much to the dismay and disgust of state officials. Those credited with the Gads Hill (also spelled Gadshill) train robbery were the members of the James-Younger Gang.

In 1874, Gads Hill was a community with a population of around thirty and was located 130 miles south of St. Louis in Wayne County. On the afternoon of Saturday, January 31, five men wearing masks rode into town and headed straight for the railroad station. On arriving, they took control without firing a shot. The station manager was ordered to raise the appropriate flag to alert the engineer of the soon-to-arrive Little Rock Express to divert the train to the siding. This manner of getting a train to stop became a *modus operandi* for the James-Younger Gang.

When the train pulled to a stop, two of the outlaws climbed into the locomotive cab and held the engineer and fireman at gunpoint. Using the two railroad employees as hostages, gang members broke into the mail and express cars. The amount of money taken from these cars was never determined for certain. Reports ranged from $2,000 to $22,000.

With the contents of the safe in hand, the robbers then went through the coaches systematically robbing the male passengers, taking money, jewelry, and watches. When finished, they mounted their horses and fled south. But before leaving, the robbers left a long and descriptive note:

> *The most daring on record—the southbound train on the Iron Moun-tain railroad was Robbed here this evening by seven heavily armed men, and robbed of ------- dollars. The robbers arrived at the station some time before the arrival of the train, and arrested the station agent and put him under guard, then threw the train on the switch. The robbers were all large men, none of them under six feet tall. They were all masked and started in a southerly direction after they had robbed the train. They were all mounted on fine blooded horses. There is a hell of an excitement in this part of the country.*

On an outside fold of the note was written: "This contains an exact account of the robbery. We prefer this to be published in the newspaper rather than the grossly exaggerated accounts that usually appear after one of our jobs."

Word of the robbery reached the larger town of Piedmont, eighteen miles south of Gads Hill. A posse was formed and sent out to the robbery site. Nothing came of this effort. However, a few days later, a reward of $17,500 was posted for the arrest and conviction of the train robbers. This served to attract the attention of a number of men ranging from profes-sional trackers to amateurs hoping to make some money.

The express company invited the Pinkerton National Detective Agency to become involved in the pursuit. John W. Witcher (also spelled Whicher), a young and aggressive detective, was sent and he eventually discerned the trail of the outlaws. It led toward the west. Witcher was followed by several armed pursuers, some professional trackers and a handful of inexperienced citizens. When it became clear that the trail led to Clay and Jackson Counties, the homes of the Jameses and Youngers, the chase was abandoned by all but Witcher. Entering Clay County was the last anyone saw the detective alive. One month later his body was found. It had been riddled with bullets.

The Pinkertons narrowed the suspects in Witcher's murder down to Jesse James and Clell Miller. During their investigation, they learned that Jesse and Frank made regular nightly rides to the family farm near Kearney, Missouri, to visit their mother and young stepbrother, Archie.

A special train transporting Pinkerton agents arrived in Clay County on January 26, 1875. The conductor of the train was a man named William Westfall (also spelled Westphal). Wasting little time, the detectives made their way to the James home, having reason to believe the outlaw brothers were inside. The Pinkertons lobbed homemade bombs through the windows, crude incendiary devices consisting of oil-soaked rags wrapped around pieces of metal. One or more of them rolled, or was kicked into, the fireplace and an explosion resulted. Archie was killed and Jesse's mother suffered a severe injury, resulting in the amputation of her right arm.

The community was outraged at the action of the Pinkertons. The head of the organization, Allan Pinkerton, was indicted for Archie's death. Because of real and implied threats against the agency, the company decided not to send any more detectives to Clay County.

Jesse James was deeply moved by the loss of his stepbrother and the injury to his mother. His penchant for revenge against the Yankee authorities grew hotter, and it would be some time before it was quelled.

MUNCIE, KANSAS

During the early days of December 1874, Jesse James, in the company of one of the Younger brothers, was hanging around Kansas City. It is believed the outlaw was observing the comings and goings of the Kansas Pacific Railroad through the city, as well as potential robbery sites along the track. He focused on the timing of an express run from Denver, Colorado, reputed to be carrying a significant amount of cash and jewelry in the safe. After discerning the routes the train would take, James directed his attention to the small town of Muncie, located a short distance west of Kansas City in Wyandotte County, Kansas.

Around 4 p.m. on December 8, five riders brandishing Navy Colts and breech-loading carbines rode up to a section line crew carrying out maintenance on the tracks at the selected site. At gunpoint, James ordered the workers to stack railroad ties and rails on the track.

Within an hour, the outlaws heard the oncoming train. James ordered one of the section hands to take a position far ahead of the stacked crossties and rails and wave down the train. Once the KP train came to a halt, two of the outlaws held guns on the engineer and fireman while the remainder broke into the express car. Inside they encountered the express car messenger, Frank Webster, who put up a brief resistance but was quickly subdued. The outlaws ordered Webster to unlock the safe, but he refused. They asked again, explaining that if he didn't, they would kill him. Convinced, Webster unlocked the safe and the robbers removed an estimated $27,000 in currency and a container of gold dust valued at $5,000.

One of the outlaws robbed passengers of watches, but James instructed him to return them, explaining that they were "not after personal property."[4] When the job was completed, the outlaws mounted up and rode away.

The initial reports of the holdup implicated the James-Younger Gang. Several days later, Kansas City police arrested Bud McDaniel, known to have ridden with Jesse and Frank James. At the time of his arrest, McDaniel had in his possession $1,000 in cash along with several pieces of jewelry. The jewelry was identified as having been taken during the KP train robbery. Before McDaniel could be brought to trial, though, he escaped. Later, he was killed by a farmer near Lawrence, Kansas. Law enforcement authorities never caught up with any other member of the James-Younger Gang.

As with a number of robberies associated with Jesse James, some controversy exists relative to whether or not he was present at the Muncie holdup. A small cadre of James researchers are convinced the outlaw did not participate in the robbery but was instead in Nashville, Tennessee, at the time, where his wife, Zerelda, was giving birth to their son, Jesse Edwards James.

GLENDALE, MISSOURI

The 1879 Glendale train robbery allegedly perpetrated by Jesse James and his gang has been described in books, articles, and even song. Like a lot of events linked to the famous outlaw, this one is also layered with controversy: Was Jesse James behind the robbery or was it a different gang?

Glendale, Missouri, is located in Jackson County, a short distance east of Kansas City. A band of suspicious looking riders led, it is believed by most, by Jesse and Frank James, entered Glendale around sunset on October 8, 1879. They rode into the small community as if expecting no resistance whatsoever. They were surprised to find a number of men gathered in front of the general store, all apparently farmers, and all apparently edgy at the appearance of suspicious looking strangers in their small village. As the newcomers rode up, they drew their weapons and ordered the farmers to make their way down the street to the train station.

Once at the station, the outlaws cut the telegraph wires. At gunpoint, they forced the station agent to change the track signal from green to red. If red, it communicated to the engineer of an oncoming train that it was necessary to stop.

The southbound Chicago and Alton Railroad express was scheduled to pass through the station at 8 p.m., so when the train slowed and pulled to a stop, the express car messenger grew concerned. He knew the pause was unscheduled and became apprehensive. Expecting the worst, he opened the safe, pulled the money from it, and stuffed it into a nearby satchel. This done, the messenger attempted to exit the express car by climbing out a window but was spotted by the outlaws. They seized the frightened man and pistol-whipped him.

After breaking into the express car, the outlaws went to the open safe and found money that had escaped the notice of the messenger. Initial reports of the robbery stated that $40,000 was taken, but a subsequent investigation revealed that the amount was only $6,000. It was the illegal custom among most railroads during these times to report losses greater than what actually occurred, in an attempt to make money off the insurance companies. In addition to the cash, the robbers also took a number of what they presumed to be valuable bank notes, but which turned out to be worthless.

Before riding away from the scene of the robbery, the outlaws left a note that read: "We are the boys who are hard to handle, and we will make it hot for the boys who try to take us." The message contained two signatures—Jesse and Frank James.

The note has been in dispute almost from the time it was found. Some researchers claim it is authentic, others insist it was not penned by either of the James brothers.

Here are some facts: Jesse James was spotted in nearby Kansas City during the days prior to the robbery. In addition, there were eyewitnesses at and near the scene of the crime who insisted the leader of the gang was Jesse. Despite this evidence, the general manager of the US Express Company initiated a press release that stated it was *not* the James Gang that was involved in the robbery. His reasons for the statement were never explained.

One year later, a known James associate named Tucker Bassham was apprehended and charged as a participant in the Glendale train robbery. Under questioning, Bassham stated that the gang was indeed led by Jesse James. Later, a second suspect, Dick Liddil, was arrested, and he related the same information.

WINSTON, MISSOURI

For a time during late 1879 and most of 1880, many were convinced that the outlaw Jesse James was dead. A rumor made its way throughout much of Missouri that he had been killed by one of his gang members during an argument. Proof of his demise, however, was not forthcoming. All doubts about the health of James were dispelled on July 15, 1881, when he led his band into Winston, Missouri, for the purpose of robbing a Chicago, Rock Island & Pacific passenger express train.

Winston was a tiny Daviess County community southwest of Gallatin. At 7 p.m., as the train slowly pulled away from the station, six men ran out of hiding and climbed aboard. While four of them entered one of the passenger coaches, two climbed to the roof of the car, made their way forward, crossed the express car and tender, and dropped into the engine cab, surprising the engineer and fireman. At gunpoint, the engineer was ordered to advance the train some distance up the track to a preselected location. On reaching a remote section of the track, he was ordered to pull the train to a halt.

Once the train was stopped, two of the robbers broke into the express car but found only $600 in cash. It has been argued among James researchers that robbery was not the primary motivation for stopping the train, but rather the assassination of a man known to be on board. In one of the coaches, the passengers were being held up—money, watches, and jewelry were taken. One of the outlaws, presumably Jesse James, stepped up to the conductor and, without preamble, shot him down. Passengers who witnessed the event stated that the conductor remained passive during the entire robbery and merely stood with his hands raised. It was later learned that he was William Westfall, the conductor of the train that carried the Pinkerton detectives to Clay County when they firebombed the James home, killing stepbrother Archie and severely injuring Jesse's mother. Revenge? Coincidence? The incident is debated to this day.

The manner in which the train was boarded and stopped represented a significant departure from the usual routine in which the James Gang robbed trains. It has been argued that this particular train was boarded and stopped for the express purpose of killing conductor Westfall.

Though there is a certain outlaw and revenge logic in the above, this train robbery, like many others associated with Jesse and Frank James, remains controversial in that some researchers have taken the position that the brothers were never involved. The growing mystery and elusiveness related to the participation of Jesse and Frank is likely just the way they wanted it.

BLUE CUT, MISSOURI

Blue Cut, Missouri, is a location two miles west of Glendale Station, a short distance outside Kansas City. Blue Cut, sometimes referred to as Rocky Cut, was sliced out of a steep slope. The tracks served both the Chicago and Alton Railroad and the Missouri Pacific Railroad. The site was remote and favored by train robbers as an ideal spot for a holdup, since the trains had to slow down in negotiating the winding cut. In fact, at least three train robberies occurred here. The first was perpetrated by Jesse and Frank James and gang.

On September 7, 1881, the engineer of the eastbound train spotted warning lanterns waving in the distance. As the train slowed, both the engineer and the fireman noted that the tracks had been blocked with a pile of heavy logs and rocks. When the train halted, three of the robbers wasted no time in breaking into the express car while the rest fired their weapons into the passenger cars to inhibit interference.

On entering the express car, the outlaws were disappointed at what they found, estimated to be between $1,000 and $3,000. Angered, they attacked the express car messenger, striking him repeatedly with their revolvers. A subsequent investigation revealed that the outlaws mistakenly selected the wrong train to rob; the one following several minutes behind was transporting $100,000. While some of the outlaws were in the express car, others were robbing Frank Burton, the brakeman. After the outlaws took his valuables and walked away, Burton turned and raced back up the tracks to wave down the second train, preventing it from slamming into the one that had been stopped.

After mounting up, the men also passed the second train. One of the outlaws, a man described as the leader of the gang, saluted the engineer of that train and passed him $2 from the stolen cash, telling him to "drink to the health of Jesse James."[5]

Like the robbery of the Chicago, Rock Island, & Pacific Railroad in Adair, Iowa, the participation of Jesse and Frank James in the Blue Cut event came into question. Over the course of several weeks, several suspects in the crime were arrested and charged, none of whom had even been part of the James Gang. A short time later, two members of the gang were captured, and both of them swore that Jesse and Frank had led the raid.

According to the bulk of recorded history, Jesse James was shot and killed in St. Joseph, Missouri, on April 3, 1882, by sometime gang member Robert Ford. As with many of the events associated with the life of Jesse James, his death ultimately generated additional controversy. Little time had passed before rumors circulated that it was not Jesse who was killed, but that it was all a scheme to allow the wanted outlaw to vanish. According to some, the body of a look-alike relative who had died two days earlier was substituted.

Arguments were waged from both sides of the issue. Over the years a handful of men who came forth claiming to be Jesse James were subsequently dismissed as imposters. Still, the rumors persisted that the outlaw was still alive. In spite of a disinterment of the alleged bones of Jesse James accompanied by an examination of the DNA, the controversy has not been put to rest, which is exactly the way Jesse James would have wanted it.

Sam Bass

3

Sam Bass

At a time early in his outlaw career, Sam Bass and his companions decided to rob a Union Pacific train at Big Springs, Nebraska. The attempt was successful, and the amount of money taken was impressive. It was enough to encourage the brigand to pursue this dangerous and illegal occupation further. A short time later, Bass traveled to Texas and began to explore similar opportunities. Sam Bass, in fact, introduced train robbery to the Lone Star State.

Sam Bass was born into a large family on a farm near Mitchell in southern Indiana on July 21, 1851. (At least one writer provides the date of July 2, 1851.) When he was but a small child, Sam's mother passed away. An older brother who enlisted in the Union Army was killed at the Battle of Richmond in 1862. Sam, along with his siblings, pitched in and helped his father with the hard work and long hours associated with maintaining a farming livelihood. By all accounts, the farm prospered.

When his father died in 1864, thirteen-year-old Sam went to live with his uncle, Dave Sheeks. Sheeks was regarded by his neighbors as wealthy and owned a number of large farms and sawmills in the vicinity. During his time in Indiana, Bass toiled on the Sheeks farms but never received any education. He was able to read only a few words and could barely sign his name. While he was a hard and dependable worker, farming held little appeal to the young Bass, and he began making plans to head out west at the first opportunity.

While he growing up, Bass heard stories about the Reno Gang, a band of bank, stagecoach, and train robbers who operated throughout much of Indiana and Illinois. The Reno Gang is credited with the first peacetime robbery of a train on October 6, 1866, in Seymour, Indiana, forty miles northeast of Mitchell. The robbers, holding the express car messenger at gunpoint, took $12,000 from the safe and got away with no difficulty. An escapade such as this appeared to offer far more adventure and excitement, not to mention income, than what young Sam was experiencing on the farm.

From travelers who stopped at the Sheeks farms, Bass heard stories of the American West, stories of cowboys, buffalo hunters, and Indian fighters. He was known to have expressed his desire to journey westward to see for himself what adventures might lie there. It was said he once mentioned to an acquaintance that he might take up robbing trains like the Reno Gang.

Bass left home at around eighteen years of age. One of his first stops was Rosedale, Mississippi. In need of money, he found work as a farm laborer for a time.

While in Rosedale, according to one biographer, Bass learned to shoot a gun and play cards. By all accounts, he was a decent shot with a revolver but a terrible poker player.

From Rosedale, Bass moved on to Arkansas, and then to North Texas, hitching a ride with a family traveling in a covered wagon and eventually arriving in Denton County some time in 1870. Bass had no trouble finding employment on nearby ranches. His commitment to his tasks impressed those around him, and he was regarded by all who knew him as responsible and frugal. As with farming, Bass soon learned he had no love for working on ranches.

Bass left the ranch work and went to live in the town of Denton. He found work at times as a stable boy, a handyman, and driving a freight wagon.

By the time he was an adult, Sam Bass was five feet six inches tall. He had grown lean and muscular from hard work. His posture was a bit stooped, which gave the impression that he was much older. With his black hair and deep black eyes, he was often mistaken for an American

Indian. According to researchers, Bass was somewhat careless in his personal appearance; it was said he seldom bathed or shaved except when posing for the rare photograph.

Bass's biographers have written that he rarely showed any interest in female company. As far as is known, Bass was never romantically or otherwise linked with a woman during his lifetime.

One of Bass's interests was horses, and he grew adept at raising, training, and breeding them. His desire was to generate a stock of good racing horses, and in time he developed into a skillful breeder. Whenever Bass had the opportunity, he traveled around the countryside entering his animals in racing competitions. In addition to Denton, he raced in Dallas, Fort Worth, Grandbury, Waco, San Antonio, and other locations in Texas, as well as in Oklahoma. He won more than he lost. When not racing his horses, Bass spent his time drinking and gambling.

During his time of raising and racing horses, Bass found himself in trouble with the law on occasion. In one case he was charged with doping his horses. In another, he was alleged to have cheated an opponent out of a race by intimidating the judges.

After a few weeks of racing his famed "Denton mare" in San Antonio, Bass fell in with a man named Joel Collins. Collins was a former saloon owner who spent a lot of his time at the horse races. Like Bass, Collins had had a few scrapes with the law. He was described as a "violent, reckless man who had killed a Mexican or two. . . ."[1]

While racing and training horses, Bass accumulated a few head of cattle, as did Collins. At one point, Collins suggested they combine their herds, drive them to Dodge City, Kansas, and sell them. In 1876, Bass and Collins, along with three other cowhands, drove the herd northward. By the time they had arrived at Dodge City, the herd was considerably larger than when they left Texas, leading biographers to speculate that more cattle were obtained along the trail by theft. Questions of ownership arose that Bass and Collins were unable to answer satisfactorily, negating the possibilities of a sale. In response to the growing suspicions, the two men moved the herd northward to Nebraska where it was finally sold. After paying off the cowhands, Bass and Collins pocketed $8,000.

From Nebraska, Bass and Collins continued northward into Dakota Territory, eventually arriving in the town of Deadwood. There, they invested their money in a freight company, a zinc mine, and a whorehouse. Between the hard drinking and compulsive gambling, neither Bass nor Collins could focus on their enterprises long enough to make a go of them, and eventually they all folded.

Following one business failure after another, Bass and Collins met Jack Davis, a fellow gambler. Davis, who had experience robbing stagecoaches, pointed out that shipments of gold from the mines were done by stagecoach. The coaches, explained Davis, moved along seldom-traveled roads in remote parts of the countryside, offering a number of real and potential locations for a holdup. To the three men, robbing stages seemed like a logical way to make some money and provide an easier way to make a living. A handful of additional men were added to the gang and plans were formulated to rob a coach. So broke were Bass, Collins, and the others, that they were forced to steal horses and saddles in order to perpetrate the holdup.

For Bass and Collins, the occasional stagecoach robbery kept them in money, and the money kept them in alcohol and at the gaming tables. This was not to last, however, for the area law enforcement, seeking to put a stop to the holdups, was closing in on the two men.

Enraged by the killing of a stagecoach driver during one of the robberies, lawmen were determined to end the reign of terror along the roads and bring the criminals to justice. Sensing this, Bass and Collins, along with gang members Jack Davis, Jim Berry, Tom Nixon, and Bill Heffridge, decided it was time to leave the Dakotas and travel south. Along the way, they decided to rob a train in Nebraska.

BIG SPRINGS, NEBRASKA

On the evening of September 18, 1877, Sam Bass and his gang held up a Union Pacific train in the tiny community of Big Springs, twenty miles west of Ogallala, in western Nebraska. The Big Springs theft ushered in Bass's short but effective and colorful career as a train robber. While the robbery was attributed to the Bass gang, some researchers believe that Joel Collins was the mastermind of the plot.

With guns drawn, Bass and five companions entered the station and secured it, taking the lone stationmaster, George Barnhart, prisoner. Barnhart was forced to stand beside the tracks and wave a red lantern, a signal to the engineer of the arriving train to pull to a stop. Moments later, the outlaws cut the telegraph lines.

Within an hour the scheduled train arrived and chugged to a halt. When engineer George Vroman spotted the armed riders, he began throwing coals at them. His response was quickly quelled with a few shots from the bandits. Once Vroman was subdued, the outlaws climbed into the cab of the locomotive and neutralized him and the fireman. They doused the firebox with water so the train could not proceed.

Following this, Bass and Collins walked down the tracks, identified the express car, and forced the express messenger, George Miller, to open the door. Miller explained that the safe had a combination lock and that he did not have the code. The safe, Miller explained, could be opened only by certain agents at specific points along the line. The outlaws accepted Miller's story and contented themselves with going through bags and boxes. In a short time they found three wooden boxes, each containing $20,000 in uncirculated gold pieces. While this was going on, Davis, Berry, Nixon, and Heffridge went through the passenger coaches taking money and valuable items.

Moments later, the train robbers made their getaway with $60,000 in $20 gold pieces, all fresh from the San Francisco mint, along with $500 in cash. Before departing, one of the gang members pistol-whipped the freight agent, and one passenger suffered a light head wound when he was shot for not complying with the bandits' orders. The six outlaws rode away from the holdup eager to spend their newfound riches. At the time, it represented the biggest haul from a train robbery in history.

After fleeing the scene of the robbery, some of the gang members talked about the advantages of traveling to South America, a popular destination for American outlaws at the time who were feeling the pressure of the law closing in on them. There was little agreement to this plan, and the gang members decided to split up. Joel Collins and Bill Heffridge rode away to Kansas. Jim Berry and Tom Nixon traveled to Kansas City, Missouri. Sam Bass, accompanied by Jack Davis, headed for Texas.

Initially law enforcement authorities believed the Big Springs train had been robbed by the Jesse James Gang, which by this time had gained a major reputation. Following an intense investigation, it was later determined it had been perpetrated by a gang consisting of Bass and Collins along with four other men whose identities at the time were unknown.

Not long after arriving in Kansas, Collins and Heffridge made plans to rob a Kansas Pacific Railroad train at Buffalo Station in the west-central part of the state. On their way to the station the two outlaws encountered a squad of soldiers from Fort Hays. Riding with the troopers were several area law enforcement authorities who became suspicious of the two men. A shootout ensued, and both Collins and Heffridge were killed.

On arriving in Denton County, Texas, Bass spotted his likeness on wanted posters along with a description of his role in the Nebraska train robbery. He decided to lay low for a time, hiding out in a remote region in the northwestern corner of the county called Cove Hollow, an area with which he was already familiar.

Bass found comfort in being back in Texas. With a reward out for him, however, he realized it would be difficult to return to the rather public occupation of raising and training racehorses. He decided the best way to make a living was to continue to pursue something else he was good at—train robbery. To Sam Bass, the growing and expanding railroad businesses in Texas offered a vast array of opportunities.

ALLEN, TEXAS

Emboldened by the successful Big Springs, Nebraska, train robbery, Bass lost little time in putting together another gang. He recruited Frank "Blockey" Jackson, Seaborn Barnes, and Tom Spottswood. Other gang members who came and went during Bass's time in Texas included Henry Underwood; Arkansas Johnson; Jim Murphy; Pipes Herndon; and William Collins, a cousin of Joel Collins.

While Bass was studying his chances of pulling off another train robbery, he learned about shipments of payrolls and other monies by stagecoaches traveling into and out of Fort Worth several miles to the south. After two successful coach holdups but with not much to show for the effort, Bass once again turned his concentration toward the railroads, redoubling his efforts to determine a suitable target.

The February 22, 1878, robbery of the Houston and Texas Central passenger train in Allen, Texas, was notable for two principal reasons: It was the first recorded train robbery in the state of Texas, and it was organized and carried out by a man who would become one of Texas's most famous outlaws, Sam Bass. In fact, it was the first of four train robberies Bass was to commit in Texas before he met his end at the hands of Texas Rangers several months later.

In mid-February, Bass and his gang rode into Allen, Texas, located in Collin County, twenty-five miles north-northeast of downtown Dallas. From a hiding place in a nearby clump of trees, the outlaws observed the comings and goings of the Houston and Texas Central trains and the activities of employees at the station. Built in 1872, the H&TC Railroad was purchased by J. P. Morgan in 1877. As they watched, the gang members learned the times of arrivals and departures of the trains and the shifts and schedules of the station employees. Bass explained to his gang members how they were going to execute the robbery of the train.

On the afternoon of February 22, and only a few minutes before the arrival of the train, Bass and his gang stormed into the station and subdued the agent, the lone person on duty.

The oncoming H&TC train was not scheduled to stop, but Bass ordered the agent to alert the engineer to make certain it did. The agent offered no resistance. Once the train was flagged down and stopped, James Thomas, the express messenger, opened the express car door to ascertain the reason. When he spotted the robbers approaching the express car, Thomas retrieved his revolver and fired several shots at them. The gang immediately returned fire, but no one was hit. Thomas scrambled back into the express car, closed the door, and locked it.

When Bass reached the car, he pounded on the door and demanded it be opened. Inside the car, messenger Thomas took refuge behind some wooden trunks and prepared to resist the bandits.

The term "messenger" as applied by the railroads meant "courier." The messenger traveled in the express car, maintained the paperwork associated with what was being transported, and was, to a large degree, responsible for everything in the car. That is why most messengers were so resistant to intrusion from robbers, often refusing to open the express car door even under threat of death. Messengers were often fired when cars had been robbed.

As Bass carried on a dialog with Thomas, another gang member raced through the passenger cars shouting that a robbery was taking place and that fifty to sixty outlaws were involved. His intention was to force the passengers to seek cover and not leave the train. No one did. Bass had decided earlier not to rob or harm the passengers.

Meanwhile, back at the express car, Thomas continued to refuse to open the door. The outlaws fired their revolvers through the wooded sides and into the car, and Thomas fired back. Thomas was slightly wounded by one of the outlaw's bullets. After a few minutes, Thomas, out of ammunition and concerned about his bleeding wound, finally surrendered and opened the door. After the outlaws climbed into the express car, Bass ordered Thomas to open the safe. The messenger refused, but when Bass threatened to kill him if he didn't, he complied. From the safe, Bass removed, according to some documents, between $1,200 and $2,500. At least one other report, however, suggested that the outlaws got away with less than $500.

Moments later, with Bass in the lead, the gang mounted their horses and rode toward their Cove Hollow hideout. The robbery had gone off with few complications. None of the passengers were harmed, and express messenger Thomas's wound turned out to be minor.

Two days following the Allen train robbery, hundreds of wanted posters appeared throughout the region with offers of a $1,500 reward for the capture of each of the train robbers. Gang member Tom Spottswood, whose mask had fallen from his face during the robbery, was identified by messenger Thomas and arrested. Spottswood spent two years in jail while his case was in and out of the courts. He was finally acquitted.

Sam Bass and the rest of his gang retreated to the Cove Hollow hideout where they remained out of sight for several weeks. The outlaws spent their time playing cards. Encouraged with his success and the ease with which the Allen, Texas, holdup was accomplished, Sam Bass immediately began making plans for his next train robbery. He decided it would take place just over three-and-a-half weeks later in Hutchins, Texas.

Local sheriff departments directed some of their attention to train schedules and kept themselves informed of valuable shipments. Meanwhile, the Texas Rangers began to take an interest in Sam Bass and his gang of train robbers. Not much more time would pass before these two entities would collide with one another.

HUTCHINS, TEXAS

Sam Bass had grown convinced that robbing trains was an effective and efficient way to make a living. Thus far in his life, save for some horse racing victories, train robbery was the only thing with which he'd ever had measurable success, and that apparently appealed to and satisfied his oft-stated craving for adventure. He wanted to match the excitement of his Big Springs, Nebraska, holdup, and he longed to ride away with a similar impressive amount of loot. To Sam Bass, train robbery was certainly easier and more lucrative than farming and ranching, and it provided for greater excitement. Convinced he could outsmart and elude pursuit by area lawmen with little difficulty, the outlaw wasted no time in planning another holdup.

Bass determined that the chances for success were greater by conducting the robberies at small town train stations; there would be fewer witnesses, the stations were generally manned by only one employee at a time, and law enforcement was often negligible to nonexistent. Since robbing trains was unheard of in Texas until the incident with the Union Pacific train at Allen less than a month earlier, Bass knew well that lawmen were unprepared for such and unpracticed in pursuit. After familiarizing himself with potential targets and train schedules, Bass decided to pull his next job at Hutchins, a tiny community located ten miles southeast of Dallas.

According to information gleaned by Bass, the Houston and Texas Central Railroad's No. 4 train would arrive at the Hutchins station at 10 p.m., March 18, 1878. Following the procedure established during the Big Springs, Nebraska, robbery as well as the recent heist in Allen, Bass and his gang burst into the Hutchins station with guns drawn. The surprised and frightened stationmaster was tied up and placed in a closet. Minutes before the H&TC No. 4 arrived, the outlaws assembled on the depot loading platform.

After the train pulled to a stop, Bass led his companions to the locomotive, climbed into the cab, and he and Frank Jackson ordered the engineer and fireman to raise their hands and step out onto the dock at gunpoint. As Bass busied himself questioning the engineer relative to what sort of monies were being transported in the express car, the Texas Express Company Agent Heck Thomas opened the express car door and stepped down to the ground, unaware the train was about to be robbed. He was joined by the mail car clerk, a man named Terrell. As the two men engaged in conversation, they looked up and spotted the engineer and fireman with raised hands and immediately deduced that a robbery was underway. Scrambling back into the express car, Thomas began collecting the canvas bags containing money and searched for a suitable hiding place. In the end, he crammed the bags, containing $4,000, into the large potbellied stove and the stovepipe. Terrell raced to the nearby mail car and did his best to hide what he determined were valuable shipments.

Moments later, Bass and his gang arrived at the express car and instructed Thomas to hand over the money bags. Thomas resisted, shots were fired, and the agent suffered bullet wounds to the face and neck.

During the confrontation at the express car, the train conductor, accompanied by the brakeman, ran through the passenger coaches warning of the robbery taking place and enlisting help from any of the male passengers who were armed. Several men gathered at the coach windows, lowered them, and began firing at the outlaws standing outside the express car, forcing them to take shelter.

Frustrated, Bass threatened to shoot the fireman if Thomas did not turn over the money. The agent surrendered and complied, handing over to Bass an amount of money that he had earlier set aside from the larger bags of cash. With a portion of the loot in hand and no indication of acquiring any more, Bass and his gang, still being harassed by the shooting from the passengers, decided to forego an attempt on the mail car and made a hasty retreat. Making their way back to the horses, they mounted up and rode away to the east.

A posse of several volunteers was quickly put together and set off in pursuit of the outlaws. After riding hard for two miles, Bass and his gang arrived at the banks of the Trinity River. Without pausing, they turned north and headed for the Cave Hollow hideout in Denton County. The posse tracked the gang to the river but lost their trail a short time later. Following a fruitless effort to relocate it, they decided to return to Hutchins.

Sam Bass was angry and disappointed with the haul from the H&TC train No. 4. It amounted to far less than the take from the Allen train robbery. Most estimates suggest the gang made off with only $500, but one report placed the amount at a mere $89.

Rather than linger on this discouraging development, Bass regarded the botched Hutchins train robbery as little more than a fluke, the result of bad luck, and no fault of his own. He was still convinced that robbing trains was the quickest and easiest path to wealth, and he began making plans to undertake another as soon as possible. He set his sights on Eagle Ford, Texas.

EAGLE FORD, TEXAS

Just over two weeks after his last train robbery, Sam Bass decided it was time to try another. For his next undertaking, he and his gang targeted the Texas and Pacific Railroad and decided to hold it up when it arrived at midnight at the Eagle Ford Station on April 4, 1878. Eagle Ford was located six miles west of downtown Dallas. After making their plans, the gang left their Denton County hideout in Cove Hollow and, traveling along back roads to avoid being seen by lawmen, made their way to the small community.

Bass was confident in his method, but apparently suffered from a bit of complacency. He had little respect or regard for the railroads or, for that matter, law enforcement. He was convinced he was smarter and tougher than all of them and perceived them as only a minor and easily overcome obstacle to his goals. Bass's attitude and overconfidence were soon to encounter some difficulties.

Unknown to Bass, the railroads and the express companies were developing strategies to deal with robbers and robberies. Since express cars were the obvious targets of the bandits, the companies decided on alternatives. One method developed to foil the bandits was to place money in a bag carried by an agent or agents who traveled as passengers and rode in the coaches. In the case of the T&P train set to arrive at the Eagle Ford station, the agent was a woman. In the past, the Sam Bass gang never bothered the passengers, and remained particularly deferential to the women.

The robbery was routine and followed the pattern of the previous two. The outlaw gang—composed of Bass, Arkansas Johnson, Seaborn Barnes, and one other unidentified man—met little to no resistance from the stationmaster or the express company messenger and guard. After breaching the express car, the outlaws were simply handed a small bag containing some money by the frightened and timid express messenger. No shots were fired the entire time. When the express company later learned that the messenger, as well as the guard, offered no resistance whatsoever to the outlaws, it terminated them.

After Bass and his gang had ridden what they perceived to be a safe distance from the robbery site, they stopped to camp for the night. After counting the money and finding it to consist of only a handful of bills, Bass began to suspect he may have been duped and that he had been made to believe he had conducted a successful robbery and had gotten away with it when, in truth, the bulk of the money shipment had been concealed elsewhere. When Bass finally understood he had escaped with only a token amount of money, he realized he and his gang were victims of a ruse, one perpetrated either by the railroad or the express company. Try as he might, Bass was at a loss to understand how it had happened.

Following the unsuccessful robbery, the outlaws once again mounted up and returned to the Denton County hideout. More than ever, Sam Bass was determined to make a big haul from a train robbery, and the sooner the better. He began planning his next one, and vowed to be more alert this time.

MESQUITE, TEXAS

Sam Bass's fourth train robbery in less than three months was not long in coming. Despite the fact that the Eagle Ford holdup was still fresh in the minds of the outlaws, the railroad companies, the express companies, and the area law enforcement personnel, the bold bandits decided to strike again. This time, they targeted a Texas and Pacific passenger train. Bass determined that the ideal location for the robbery would be Mesquite, Texas.

Mesquite proved to offer a considerably different situation than the three previous robberies. Unlike the others, which occurred in small communities, Mesquite was a sizable town located twelve miles east of downtown Dallas that boasted numerous residences, a general store, a blacksmith, churches, schools, and saloons.

On April 10, 1879, Sam Bass and his gang, now consisting of Seaborn Barnes, Albert Herndon, Frank Jackson, Arkansas Johnson, Sam Pipes, Henry Underwood, and another unidentified man, all armed and masked, burst into the train station, subdued the agent, and trussed him up. This done, the gang members sat down to await the arrival of the T&P train.

To this point, Bass's approach to robbing trains had followed a pattern, one that had proven successful. Thus far, the heists had all worked according to plan and the outlaw saw no reason to change. On this attempt, however, Bass and his gang were to encounter more resistance than during previous ones, resistance for which they were unprepared.

When the train finally arrived, Frank Jackson climbed into the locomotive cab and held the engineer and fireman at gunpoint. A moment later, he ordered them to step out onto the platform. As Bass led the rest of the gang toward the express car, he was met with the unexpected—the messenger, J. S. Kerley.

When the train stopped, Kerley opened the express car door and was preparing to drop off a package when he discerned that a robbery was about to take place. As the outlaws approached the express car, Kerley produced a handgun and opened fire on them. Though no one was struck, Bass and his gang members ducked for cover.

While Bass was deciding what to do next, Kerley used the opportunity to slam the express car door shut and lock it. Inside with Kerley were two guards, both armed. Reloading his handgun, the messenger took up a defensive position and prepared to protect the shipment from the bandits. While he was waiting for events to unfold, Kerley decided to hide the money. He stuffed canvas bags filled with bills and coins into the express car's stovepipe and the potbellied stove. One estimate had the shipment at $1,500, however, some reports claimed the train was carrying more than $30,000.

Bass and gang were not prepared for the resistance from the messenger. They were likewise startled by the intrusion of the T&P conductor, a Civil War veteran named Julius Alvord. Upon spotting Bass and his compatriots moving toward the express car, Alvord pulled a Derringer from his pocket and began firing at them from a passenger car. The Derringer had little effect other than amusing the outlaws. Alvord threw down the Derringer, secured a revolver, and began shooting anew. One of the outlaws responded by returning fire and subsequently wounding the conductor in the shoulder. Cursing the shooter, Alvord threw down his weapon, climbed from the coach, and marched into the adjacent town screaming for a doctor to come and tend to his wound.

In addition to the express messenger and the conductor, the outlaws also came under fire from the baggage clerk, B. F. Caperton. Caperton pulled a shotgun from a large canvas pack, slid the baggage car door open a few inches, and fired away, forcing the robbers to seek cover once again. Added to this, a youth selling newspapers and candy in the passenger car secured a revolver and also began firing at the outlaws. Bass called out to the boy, admonishing him for his interference, and sent him away.

In order to remove themselves from the line of fire, the engineer and fireman dashed from the platform and took refuge beneath a nearby trestle. From this point, they watched the goings-on in relative safety.

Around the same time, new opposition to the train robbers appeared from yet another direction. On a siding not far away sat a special car filled with prison convicts assigned to construction labor. Accompanying the prisoners was a contingent of guards, all heavily armed. After observing the activity near the express car of the recently arrived T&P train, the guards opened fire on Bass and his gang of train robbers. Seaborn Barnes was hit in both legs and went down in great pain. Sam Pipes was struck in the side.

Apparently deciding not to use all their ammunition on the train robbers and thus provide the convicts an opportunity to take advantage, the guards ceased firing after only a few minutes.

Frustrated at not gaining access to the express car, Bass ran back to the locomotive and procured a can of kerosene. Though he was fired upon from different directions, he made it back to the car and pushed the can of kerosene through the narrow opening of the door. He shouted to the men inside that he was going to set the entire car afire if they did not surrender at once and come out. At first, the occupants of the car refused to budge, but when Bass doused the wooden door with the liquid and they heard him strike a match, they quickly voiced their agreement to throw down their weapons and vacate the express car.

The resistance to the train robbers wasn't done, however. As the occupants of the express car climbed to the ground, a local storekeeper arrived on the scene brandishing a pistol. He spotted the fireman hiding behind the trestle and, mistaking him for Sam Bass, forced him from his place of concealment at gunpoint. This done, the storekeeper announced to everyone within hearing distance that he had captured Sam Bass. Laughter immediately broke out, mostly among the outlaws, with none laughing as hard as Bass himself.

With the express car vacated, Bass and the others climbed in only to find themselves unable to locate any of the money bags. By the time Bass decided it was time to affect an escape, they had accumulated less than $200.

Leaving the express car, Bass and his companions helped the wounded Barnes and Pipes onto their horses. As the two bleeding men were secured in their saddles, the express messenger approached Bass and asked the outlaw leader to write out a receipt for the money he had taken from the express car. Ignoring the messenger, Bass mounted up and, leading his men, rode away.

The wounded Pipes and Herndon did not accompany the rest of the gang to the hideout in Denton County. Instead, they were dropped off at the farm of some friends outside of Dallas where they planned to rest and recuperate.

A few days later, however, Captain June Peak, leading a contingent of Texas Rangers, arrived at the farm and arrested the two outlaws. Peak had been tracking the train robbers since only a few hours following the robbery. Pipes and Herndon were charged with mail robbery, a federal crime. They were transported to Tyler, Texas, and locked into the city jail to await trial.

On April 8, Captain Peak and a squad of some thirty Texas Rangers arrived in Denton with warrants for Bass and other members of the gang. Denton Sheriff Eagan also deputized several local citizens, and together the lawmen traveled to Cove Hollow in search of Bass and his gang. On arriving, shots were exchanged, and the outlaws fled deeper into the woods.

With four train robberies in less than three months, the area newspapers were filled with articles that spoke of the growing menace of outlaws. Author Walter Prescott Webb wrote that the train robberies "furnished the state more exciting news than it had known since Lee surrendered."[2] Fearing a plague of outlawry, businessmen, bankers, and travelers armed themselves or placed weapons such that they could be conveniently retrieved in case of an emergency.

Throughout the north Texas region, passenger fares were down with travelers expressing fear that they would be robbed. Businesses and banks, not trusting the abilities of the express companies and US Mail to protect their shipments, looked for alternative ways in which to send money and bonds. Private detectives and bounty hunters arrived in Dallas offering their services to go after the train robbers. US Marshal Stillwell H. Russell was put up at a Dallas hotel along with nineteen special deputies. Pinkerton detectives swarmed Denton and Dallas Counties in search of Sam Bass and his gang. The governor of Texas sent Major John B. Jones and a company of Texas Rangers to Dallas to investigate the robberies. A rumor spread that the Sam Bass gang numbered eighty men. Rewards in excess of $8,000 were offered.

Warrants for Sam Bass, Seaborn Barnes, Frank Jackson, Arkansas Johnson, and Henry Underwood were issued. For the next several weeks,

Bass and his gang remained on the run, mostly hiding out in Cove Hollow. While Bass himself may have had a yearning to attempt more train robberies, he was now occupied with surviving, with staying ahead of the law. With the expanding and intensified pursuit from Texas Rangers and other lawmen, it was beginning to look like a race he couldn't win.

THE END OF SAM BASS

From his first train robbery at Big Springs, Nebraska, to his last in Mesquite, Texas, Sam Bass had gone from being merely a suspect to a wanted outlaw, one now pursued across a great swath of the Lone Star State. The railroads and express companies began applying pressure to the area, state, and federal law enforcement agencies, and before long, wanted posters for Bass and his gang had been tacked up throughout much of north and central Texas. The outlaws were constantly on the run and lawmen were closing in.

Throughout the spring and summer of 1878, the Sam Bass gang remained just out of reach of pursuing posses, taking refuge in the Cove Hollow hideout not far from where their leader spent several years of his young adulthood. After a time, the gang fled from the sanctuary in northwestern Denton County and made their way along back roads into the wooded and marshy Hickory Creek region in the secluded southern part of the county. Even with the Texas Rangers and local sheriff's posse nipping at their heels, the gang would manage to rob a stagecoach now and then, efforts that kept them in enough money to purchase provisions, supplies, and ammunition.

At times, the pursuing lawmen drew close enough to engage the outlaws in gun battles. During one encounter at the Warner Jackson farm near Bullard's Mill, located a few miles north of the city of Denton, three of the gang members suffered wounds, but were able to ride away. The following morning, they rode into the small town of Bolivar where they purchased fresh horses, new clothes, a supply of food, and several boxes of cartridges.

On June 13, Bass and his men were camped at Salt Creek in Wise County, about twenty-five miles west of Denton. Believing they were temporarily safe from pursuit, the outlaws were taken by surprise at the arrival of a force of some forty men consisting of Texas Rangers and members of a local posse. During the ensuing shootout, Arkansas Johnson was killed. Henry Underwood was badly wounded but managed to climb onto his horse and escape. During the melee, Bass and three other outlaws snuck away. They hid in a nearby cave while the lawmen searched for them. Sometimes they came so close that their conversations could be heard by the bandits. Sometime during the night, Bass and his companions slipped away.

On July 18, Bass and three gang members, including Frank Jackson, Seaborn Barnes, and Jim Murphy, rode into Round Rock, Texas, located about two hundred miles south of Denton. Constantly on the run and short of money, Bass had earlier made plans to rob the bank at Round Rock. Unknown to Bass, however, gang member Jim Murphy had turned informant.

Murphy, who had earlier been arrested for train robbery and was awaiting trial, was approached by law enforcement authorities and offered a deal. If Murphy would agree to betray Bass, he would spare himself a long sentence in a federal prison. Murphy capitulated. It was agreed the prosecutors would announce that Murphy had skipped bond when, in truth, he was released to rejoin Bass and the gang.

The gang members were suspicious of the furtive Murphy, and although not knowing for sure he had betrayed them, they called him a traitor, and Seaborn Barnes urged Bass to kill him. Bass confronted Murphy. who unconvincingly professed loyalty. Bass didn't believe him and had decided to kill him when Frank Jackson stepped forward and vouched for Murphy's allegiance. Bass decided to spare him. The decision would prove to be a fatal mistake.

As Bass and the gang rode south, they stopped at Belton where Bass sold a horse he had stolen days earlier in Waco. As this transaction was going on, Murphy seized the opportunity to steal away and send word to Texas Ranger Major John B. Jones that Bass was on his way to Round Rock to rob the bank. Jones sent a small detachment of Rangers from Austin to Round Rock to await Bass and the gang, then Jones made arrangements to join them.

Riding hard, the Rangers arrived in Round Rock and made preparations for an ambush in the event that Bass showed up. Additional Rangers had been alerted and were on their way. They were neither expecting nor ready for what turned out to be an early appearance by the outlaw and his brigands.

After riding into Round Rock on tired mounts, Bass, Jackson, and Barnes went to one end of the town to a store owned by Henry Koeppel. Murphy rode to another store at the opposite end of town. If both ends of town were found to be relatively clear and free of lawmen, the outlaws planned to rendezvous at Koeppel's Store. From there, they intended to proceed on to the bank and rob it.

As Bass, Jackson, and Barnes approached Koeppel's Store, deputy sheriff Maurice Moore spotted them, but did not recognize who they were. It appeared to Deputy Moore that one of the men, Bass, carried a holstered revolver under his coat. Moore immediately alerted another deputy nearby, A. M. Grimes, and together the two lawmen followed the gang members into the store.

Although Moore and Grimes had been advised that Sam Bass and his gang were likely to be in the area, the two lawmen did not believe the men they were about to face were them, nor did they remotely suspect that they might be dangerous. While Moore waited outside, Grimes approached Bass in the store, placed a hand over the bulge in his coat, and asked the newcomer if he were carrying a weapon. In response, Bass yanked the revolver from his holster and shot Grimes. As the startled deputy stumbled back toward the front door before collapsing, Moore drew his handgun and fired at Bass, striking the outlaw in the right hand, damaging the middle and ring fingers. A second later, the train robbers fled from the store, firing at deputy Moore as they ran. Moore was struck in the chest but continued shooting at the gang members.

At the first sound of the shooting at Koeppel's Store, the Texas Rangers already in town raced toward the scene. Spotting the fleeing Bass, Barnes, and Jackson, they opened fire. Ranger George Harrell took careful aim and shot Bass, the bullet striking him one inch to the left of his spinal column. Bass staggered and dropped to the ground. (Another account maintains that the crippling shot was fired by Texas Ranger Dick Ware.)

Seaborn Barnes, who had been running alongside Bass, was struck in the head and was likely dead before he hit the ground. Frank Jackson paused in his flight long enough to assist Bass to his feet. Firing his revolver at the Rangers with one hand, he used the other to assist Bass onto his horse. As the Rangers closed in, the plucky Jackson stood his ground and kept up steady fire. During a lull in the gun battle, Jackson mounted his own horse and, leading Bass's mount, rode away.

Putting his spurs to his horse, Jackson and the badly wounded Bass made their way out of Round Rock toward the north. They paused momentarily at a cemetery where they had earlier cached a rifle. After retrieving the weapon, Jackson remounted, and the two sped away once again. It was all Bass could do to stay in the saddle; he lost his grip and almost fell off his horse several times. Once out of sight of pursuit, the two outlaws turned west into dense oak woods.

Weakened from intense pain and loss of blood, Bass finally dropped from the saddle. Jackson bandaged the leader's wounds as best he could, pulled him a short distance off the trail, and tried to make him comfortable. It was clear to Jackson that Bass's wounds were serious and that the outlaw did not have long to live. Bass encouraged his partner to leave him, to escape. At first Jackson refused but was soon talked into mounting his horse and riding away. Sam Bass was now left to fend for himself. Writhing in severe pain, he lay on the ground near Brush Creek all night long, too weak to continue his flight.

By dawn, Bass had lost a considerable amount of blood. Barely able to stand, he staggered away from his hiding place. After covering nearly a half-mile, and in severe agony, he arrived at a house located not far from where a new spur of the International and Great Northern Railroad was being constructed. Several railroad workers engaged in laying track spotted Bass, barely alive, but continued with their work. They were too far away to discern that the man was badly wounded.

As Bass approached the house a woman exited the front door and saw him. She immediately noticed his blood-soaked clothing. She called to her servant girl, and as the two started to run away Bass called out to the woman, telling her he was desperately in need of a cup of water. Having difficulty speaking, he rasped out that he would go sit at the base of a nearby tree if she would send him one. The woman instructed the servant girl to deliver a cup of water to the newcomer, but by now Bass was too weak to raise the cup to his lips.

A short time later a squad of Texas Rangers searching throughout the area arrived at the railroad construction site. They saw a man lying still and quiet beneath a live oak tree, but initially mistook him for one of the railroad workers taking a nap. As the Rangers approached to investigate, Bass raised an arm and said, "Don't shoot. I'm Sam Bass."

The Rangers transported the outlaw into Round Rock and placed him in the care of a physician, though it was clear he would not live long. Texas Ranger Major John B. Jones, who had arrived at Round Rock after the shooting, sat beside Bass in the doctor's office during most of his remaining time. Jones interrogated Bass about his gang members and tried to learn information about where they might have gone into hiding. Bass was too weak to converse and lapsed into unconsciousness.

The next morning, Jones once again took a seat next to the dying Bass and questioned him further. Bass provided a bit of information on only the members of the gang who had been killed, but none at all on the survivors. He told Jones he would not betray his friends. After several minutes of conversation, Bass fell silent, then closed his eyes as if to sleep. A few moments later he opened them and looked around as if confused and frightened. He said, "The world is a-bobbin' around." Those were his last words. Sam Bass died the following day, July 21. It was his twenty-seventh birthday. He was buried in the Round Rock cemetery next to Seaborn Barnes.

Jim Murphy, whose betrayal of Sam Bass led to the outlaw's death, fled back to Denton. Word reached him that Frank Jackson was hunting him, intending to kill him for his treachery. Murphy turned himself into the Denton sheriff and requested to be placed in custody for protection. While staying at the jail, Murphy developed an eye infection. A physician gave him some medicine for the eye, cautioning him that it was for external use only. If ingested, it was toxic. Murphy committed suicide by drinking the entire contents of the vial.

With the passage of time, questions arose relative to the whereabouts of the $60,000 in gold coins stolen from the Union Pacific train at Big Springs, Nebraska. Not wanting to be caught with the freshly minted coins, Bass had buried them in four different but nearby locations at his Cove Hollow hideout. Dozens of searchers scoured the area in hopes of finding the cached loot but had no luck.

Sometime during the first decade of the 1900s, a farmer named Henry Chapman found what many believe was part of the Sam Bass treasure. Chapman owned a small farm near Springtown in Williamson County. One day as he was riding through the woods between Clear Fork Creek and Salt Creek, Chapman's mule began acting contrary. The farmer dismounted to check the girth on the balky animal and, as he was tightening it, noticed a low mound just off the trail. At first he believed it to be a grave, but closer examination revealed it was not.

Curious, Chapman dug into the mound, and only eighteen inches below the surface he was surprised to find a bushel-sized wooden box filled to the top with gold and silver coins. Each of the coins bore the mint date of 1877, matching the loot from the Big Springs, Nebraska, train robbery of that same year.

Except for this cache, none of the rest of Bass's gold coins ever appeared in circulation, supporting the belief that the remainder of the treasure is still buried intact somewhere in North Texas, awaiting discovery by some fortunate treasure hunter.

Sam Bass was a pioneer of sorts. The intrepid outlaw introduced train robbery to the state of Texas, a type of banditry unheard of in the region until his arrival. With Bass's death, train robberies in Texas halted, but only for a time. Just as railroad and law enforcement officials were beginning to breathe a bit easier, convinced that such depredations might now be a thing of the past, renewed train robbery activity burst onto the Texas scene.

4

Rube Burrow

I F S AM B ASS AND HIS SHORT-LIVED CAREER OF TRAIN ROBBERY ARE TO
be credited with introducing this form of banditry to Texas, then Rube
Burrow was the obvious heir apparent. According to the historical documents, Reuben "Rube" Burrow, along with his gang, was one of the most
prolific train robbers in the history of the United States. Though not as
well-known as Jesse James, Butch Cassidy, Sam Bass, and others, Burrow
(whose name is sometimes spelled Burrows) successfully robbed more
trains than any of them. He has been credited with eight robberies, four
of them occurring in Texas, the rest in Arkansas, Alabama, Louisiana,
and Indian Territory (now Oklahoma). Active throughout much of the
1880s and 1890s, Burrow was known as the "King of the Train Robbers,"
and was hunted by hundreds of lawmen and private detectives. He would
have added to his total of train holdups were it not for his demise at the
hands of the law.

Rube Burrow, along with his brother Jim, a prominent member of his
gang, had his origins in Lamar County, northeastern Alabama. Rube was
born Rueben Houston Burrow on December 11, 1854. Brother James
Buchanan Burrow followed in 1858. In all, ten children were the progeny
of the parents. Their father, Allen Burrow, was a successful farmer who
fought in the Civil War. He supplemented his farming income by pro-
ducing high-quality moonshine for which there grew a great demand. By
Lamar County standards, the family prospered.

Reuben's mother, Martha Terry Burrow, was known throughout the
area as an occultist and faith healer. Her clients referred to her as Dame

Rube Burrow

Burrow. People would arrive at the Burrow home from miles around to have maladies treated by Mrs. Burrow's various incantations. Her more passionate followers claimed she was able to cure arthritis, headaches, and even cancer. The more skeptical of the area citizens referred to her as a witch.

As a youth, Reuben had a tendency to get into trouble. When he was only ten years old, he shot and killed a neighbor boy, a sometime companion. Brought into court, Reuben pleaded self-defense and was acquitted. At fifteen years of age, Reuben donned a mask, broke into a neighbor's house, and stole several dollars. He was recognized and reported. On learning of this transgression, his father made him return the money.

For reasons not clear, Rube purchased a fake beard and a wig from a mail order house. When the package arrived at the post office in Jewell, Alabama, some of the hair was sticking out of one side of the box. Rube sent a friend to the post office to retrieve the package, but the postmaster, Moses J. Graves, refused to turn it over. On learning of this, an incensed Rube traveled to the post office, retrieved the package, and shot Graves through the heart. As there were no witnesses to the murder, Burrow was never arrested or charged.

In spite of the successful family farm, Rube decided early on that he was not cut out for what he regarded as the tedium and drudgery of planting, tending, and harvesting crops. Instead, like Sam Bass, he longed for adventure. He read books and articles describing the dynamic and exciting events related to the settling of the American West and was determined to see for himself.

When he was eighteen, he left the deep South and traveled to Texas. Shortly after arriving in Stephenville in 1872, he journeyed northeast to Wise County where he found employment with his Uncle Joel on a farm. Still, farming still did not satisfy his lust for adventure and he continued to search for a different outlet, as well as an income.

In addition to planting crops, Joel had a small herd of cattle, and it was to these animals that Burrow directed most of his attention. In time he became a competent cattleman and decided he wanted to own his own ranch.

The frugal Burrow saved his money and after a few years purchased a modest ranch not far from Fort Worth. For a time, he prospered, even earning a reputation as a skilled horseman. In 1876, Rube married Virginia Alverson and fathered two children. With his boyish good looks, a somewhat humble demeanor, strong work ethic, and attention to detail, he appeared to be on his way to becoming a respectable citizen.

Then calamity struck the young family. A short time after giving birth to their second child, Virginia contracted yellow fever and died a short time later. The loss of his wife appeared to have had a profound effect on Burrow. He was never the same after Virginia's death, and according to some observers, the event caused him to neglect his farm and eventually lead him down a path of lawlessness.

When he wasn't tending to the responsibilities related to his ranch, Burrow found employment with the railroads, first with Fort Worth and Denver line and later with the Texas and Pacific Railway. At least one writer has claimed that while working for the railroads, Burrow was gripped by the notion of robbing trains and how such a thing would be easy to accomplish. It has been suggested by a few researchers that Burrow was fascinated with the outlaw Jesse James and his perceived skills related to robbing trains. To Burrow, the daily grind of maintaining a horse ranch could not compare with what he perceived as the glamour and thrill of stopping a train and stealing whatever money and valuables it carried.

In 1884, brother Jim arrived in Texas and joined Reuben. In that same year, Reuben remarried, this time to Adeline Hoover. By 1886, Burrow's ranch proved unproductive, and he was unable to make a living. Shortly afterward, he and his second wife separated. Burrow, along with his brother Jim, went to work once again for Uncle Joel on another farm, this one in Erath County.

When Rube was thirty-two years old, he decided it was time to try his hand at outlawry. In addition to having been inspired earlier in his life by Jesse James, he was also impressed with the Texas train robbery activities of Sam Bass. The fact that Bass had been relentlessly pursued by law enforcement authorities and subsequently killed did not seem to deter him.

Researchers disagree on why Rube took to robbing trains. Some have suggested he found life on the farm tiresome and dull, with him barely earning enough money to pay bills and support his family. Rube himself was known to express his displeasure at such work. Others have suggested that he simply craved adventure, and that he found an outlet for this yearning in train robbery. In the end, it was adventure he found, along with an occasional heist of significant money. Today, Rube Burrow is regarded as one of Texas's most successful train robbers.

BELLEVUE, TEXAS

During a return trip to his Texas ranch from Oklahoma, Reuben and brother Jim, along with two farmhands named Henderson Bromley (sometimes spelled Brumley) and Nep Thornton, made the spontaneous decision to rob a train. According to some researchers, Rube and his companions had gone to Oklahoma on a ranch-related trip to acquire livestock. Others insist the men traveled there to rob a wealthy widow.

At 11 a.m. on the morning of December 1, 1886, Rube and his gang decided to rob a Fort Worth and Denver passenger train while it was idling at a water tank three hundred yards west of the depot in the tiny community of Bellevue, located thirty miles southeast of Wichita Falls.

Avoiding the crowd and several railroad employees milling about the depot, Rube and his gang covered their faces with bandannas and approached the locomotive from the side opposite the station so they wouldn't be seen. Thornton climbed into the cab and held the engineer and fireman at gunpoint. Rube led the other two gang members to the first passenger coach, which they boarded. With revolvers in hand, Rube announced the holdup and ordered the occupants of the cars to turn over their watches, jewelry, and money.

It is believed that the passengers had been alerted to the holdup only seconds earlier by the conductor and had ample time to hide many of their valuables under the seats before the robbers arrived. After entering each of the coaches, the three outlaws moved slowly down the aisles while instructing the passengers to remove everything from their pockets and turn the items over to them. By the time the robbers had passed through the last of the cars, they had harvested less than $300, to them a disappointing amount.

In the last car, Rube was surprised to encounter three armed soldiers who were escorting several prisoners to Fort Worth. Initially, a shootout was anticipated, but instead of resisting the robbers, the soldiers, concerned about the lives of the nearby passengers should shooting break out, allowed themselves to be disarmed. Rube and his gang members relieved the soldiers of their weapons and stuffed them into their belts. At least two of the handguns were used in later train robberies by the gang.

Rube offered to free the prisoners. At first the convicts considered it, but in the end refused. The soldiers were subsequently disciplined by their superiors for their inaction.

Since this was his first train robbery, the excitement of the undertaking, along with Rube's inexperience, caused him to completely forget about the express car, which was likely carrying several thousand dollars in cash. On the other hand, it might have been difficult to breach the express car since it was close to the station and near so many witnesses, many of whom were armed.

After riding away from the scene of the heist, Rube, though disappointed with this first effort, decided that robbing trains was where his talents lay. He also figured the payoff from a successful heist would be greater than what resulted from the hard work he invested in owning a ranch and raising cattle. Inspired by the possibilities, Rube reviewed the mistakes made during the Bellevue robbery and began making plans for the next one.

GORDON, TEXAS

Less than two months after his first successful train robbery, Rube Burrow, imbued with confidence and excited about the possibilities of acquiring a lot of money, decided to try another. For his second attempt he set his sights on the small town of Gordon, Texas, in Palo Pinto County, about seventy miles west-southwest of downtown Fort Worth. Rube learned that a Texas and Pacific train pulled into the station every day at 2 a.m., a time when few people were around to serve as witnesses or offer any resistance.

On January 23, 1887, accompanied by Henderson Bromley, Rube snuck aboard a passenger coach on the eastbound train while it was stopped at Gordon. A half-hour later, the train departed the station and proceeded down the track. When the train was several miles out of Gordon, the two outlaws left the passenger car and, revolvers in hand, scrambled up and over the coal tender, and into the cab of the locomotive.

They placed the muzzles of their weapons against the necks of the startled engineer and fireman.

Rube instructed the engineer to stop the train at a selected location another mile down the track. When the train pulled to a halt, Jim Burrow, along with Nep Thornton and a new gang member, Harrison Askew, stepped out of hiding and approached the idling engine. Askew, a hard-looking man with evil eyes, had arrived at Burrow's ranch weeks earlier seeking work. He claimed to be an ex-convict. When he learned that Rube was making plans to rob trains, he was eager to join the gang.

The engineer and fireman were ordered out of the cab at gunpoint and were marched back to the express car. On arriving, Rube hammered at the door with his fist and demanded the messenger open up with all haste. At this moment, the train conductor stepped out onto the platform of one of the passenger cars to ascertain why the train had stopped. Spotting the engineer and fireman among the group of outlaws, he called out to them, asking about the reasons for the delay. A response came in the form of a sudden volley of shots from Rube and Thornton.

From inside the express car, the frightened messenger doused his lantern. Rube hammered on the door and demanded it be opened. His order was met with silence. He repeated the demand several times but received no response. Rube then threatened to kill the engineer if the messenger did not cooperate. This threat was greeted with even more silence. Angered, and growing frustrated with the delay, Rube shot several holes in the door of the car. The response from the messenger was only more silence.

Rube had already spent more time with the robbery than intended. Tersely, he informed the messenger that if he did not open the door, they would set fire to the car, and he would be burned alive. Apparently, this threat carried more weight than the threat to kill the engineer. A few moments later, the messenger slid the door open and stepped aside, allowing Rube and Bromley to clamber into the car. Forced to comply at gunpoint, the messenger opened the safe from which the outlaw withdrew just under $3,000.

After pocketing the cash from the safe, Rube and his men, along with the messenger, engineer, and fireman, proceeded toward the mail car. After gaining entrance with less difficulty than they had experienced with the express car, they removed $2,000 from a sack of registered mail.

At this point, Askew and Bromley were sent to retrieve the horses. After stuffing the money into saddlebags, the gang mounted up. Before riding away, they fired their weapons into the air in an effort to discourage passengers and crew from exiting the coaches. Leaving the scene of the crime, the gang rode hard in a northerly direction for two hours, backtracked for several hundred yards, then turned toward the east and made their way across a stretch of rocky ground where they left no tracks.

Several hours after the robbery was reported, a posse arrived at the site of the crime. The train had not moved from the scene. After speaking with the engineer and fireman, the lawmen found the tracks of the outlaws nearby and followed them. A short time later, however, they lost the trail on the open prairie.

Rube Burrow was later identified as the leader of the train robbers, and before long wanted posters were tacked up throughout the region. Rube decided it would be prudent to lay low for a while, but his mind reeled with the possibilities of future train robberies. In time, he set his sights on a Missouri Pacific train that made a stop at McNeil, Texas.

MCNEIL, TEXAS

While Rube Burrow was biding his time at his ranch and making plans to undertake his next train heist, a gang of a dozen mysterious outlaws pulled off the robbery of a Texas and Pacific Express at the tiny village of McNeil, thirteen miles north of Austin.

The Missouri Pacific Railroad line was owned by railroad magnate Jay Gould. Around the time of the McNeil train robbery, Gould was generally recognized as the richest man in America. In addition to the Missouri Pacific, he also owned the Union Pacific, the Texas and Pacific, the Wabash, and the St. Louis, Kansas City and Northern, a tenth of all railroad lines in the United States.

Despite his wealth, or perhaps because of it, Gould was also one of the most despised men in America. His efforts to corner the US gold market in 1869 generated a stock market crash and created business panic nationwide. Gould's list of enemies was a long one, and it is believed by many that the Missouri Pacific robbery at McNeil represented an effort by somebody, or somebodies, to get back at the entrepreneur.

In addition to the railroad station, the town of McNeil boasted a dozen houses and a general store. A nearby strip mine, where lime was collected, provided employment for most of the male residents. The Missouri Pacific connected Austin with Marble Falls and Burnet, and the railroad was employed to haul large granite blocks from Marble Falls to Austin for the construction of the state capitol building.

A few minutes before 9 p.m. on the evening of May 18, 1887, ten to twelve masked, armed, and at the time unidentified men entered the McNeil train station. The outlaws held the station agent at gunpoint and walked out onto the loading platform to await the train. As the train slowed to a stop, a number of passengers rose from their seats and queued up at the door preparing to disembark. At the same time, a porter climbed down from the locomotive and walked along the tracks toward a switch he had been instructed to throw, which would allow the train to continue east toward the town of Taylor, thirty miles away. Standing near the switch was a group of rough-looking men, and as the porter approached, the strangers pulled revolvers from their holsters and began shooting in his direction. They fired over his head to frighten him, which worked well since the porter turned and scurried back toward the train.

Before the doors to the passenger cars were opened, more armed men arrived at the depot. When the travelers spotted the gunmen, they grew anxious. An instant later the outlaws fired into the coaches, forcing the passengers to take cover. Over one hundred shots were fired in only a few seconds. Windows were shattered and the sides and ceilings of the coaches were riddled with bullet holes. One passenger, a salesman named Harry Landa, was slow to take cover and suffered a bullet wound to one arm.

The train robbers had no plans to relieve the passengers of their money. They merely wanted to keep them occupied so they would not interfere with the breach of the express car, which was reported to be carrying $40,000.

With the passengers and crew cowering between the seats and on the floor, the gang moved on to the express car. When they received no response after knocking on the door, the outlaws forced it open. Inside the car they encountered two messengers who put up no resistance whatsoever. One of the robbers stepped forward, leveled a revolver at one of the messengers, a man named A. J. Nothacker, and ordered him to open the safe and hand over the money. The frightened Nothacker dutifully obeyed and handed over only one small packet of bills. Angered, the outlaw cracked Nothacker across the head with the butt of his weapon.

When the remainder of the money had been removed from the safe, the robbers turned their attention to the mailbags at the other end of the express car. Robert Spaulding, the railroad mail clerk was also on duty in the car. Spaulding decided to offer no resistance against the armed outlaws but informed them that the train was not transporting any registered mail, that it had all gone out on an earlier run. The robbers standing next to Spaulding told him that they were after Jay Gould's money, not the government's.

When the train robbers were satisfied they had accomplished all they had set out to do on this venture, they politely bade Spaulding a pleasant good evening, mounted their horses, and rode away. The amount of money taken was estimated by various officials to be between $21,000 and $55,000. Later investigations revealed that not all the money transported in the express car was taken, and it was assumed the robbers simply missed some of it among the packages, bundles, and sacks.

Law enforcement authorities were notified of the robbery as soon as possible. In Austin, a posse was formed and led by Travis County Deputy Sheriff Sam Platt and Marshal Lacy (sometimes spelled Lucy). They were joined by a Sheriff Olive. The lawmen arrived at the scene of the robbery four hours later.

The posse picked up the tracks of the train robbers shortly after arriving at the scene and tracked them to a location only one-half mile from McNeil where they had stopped to build a fire and cook a meal. Near the still warm embers of the campfire, one of the posse members found a piece of paper that tied the robbers to Joe Barber. Barber was well known to the lawmen—he had been involved in criminal activities in the past. Barber's brother, Austin, was at the time in the Huntsville prison for horse theft. Another brother, John, had recently been arrested for the same crime. Later, he would be indicted for murdering a Williamson County deputy sheriff. For several days following the robbery, reports of sightings of the gang poured into law enforcement offices from area citizens.

After a few more days, lawmen caught up with and arrested Joe Barber, James and Abner Ussery, and John and Charles Craft, and charged them with participation in the T&P holdup. The prisoners were brought before a judge who heard testimony from dozens of witnesses. In the end, the case was dismissed, and the charged men were set free.

Neither Joe Barber, the Ussery brothers, or the Craft brothers ever attempted to rob a train again. The other members of the outlaw gang were never arrested, not initially identified, and their whereabouts remained a mystery.

BENBROOK, TEXAS

Nearly six months had passed since Rube Burrow and his gang had robbed their last train. For some, in particular the railroad companies, it was like waiting for the other shoe to drop. When it finally did on June 4, 1887, few were surprised. This time, the target of Rube and his gang was the Texas and Pacific Express. The place was Benbrook, Texas, then a small community a few miles southwest of Fort Worth. Today, Benbrook is a suburb of this great city.

According to author Richard Patterson, the Benbrook train robbery is significant in that it is believed to be the first in which a railroad trestle was utilized by the outlaws to make their job easier.[1]

On the evening of June 4, the T&P Express was preparing to leave the station at Benbrook. The passengers had all boarded and were seated, the express car messenger and mail car clerk had completed their duties, and the engineer had finalized the departure protocol. When the train was only seconds from pulling away from the station, Rube Burrow and Henderson Bromley, their faces blackened with charcoal, stepped out of hiding and approached. Pulling themselves up the ladder at the rear of the tender, they climbed to the top and made their way toward the front of the car. As the train was picking up speed, the two outlaws dropped down into the cab of the locomotive, guns drawn. Rube ordered the engineer to proceed down the track, cross a deep gorge, and then stop the train on the far side of the trestle. He instructed the engineer to make certain the locomotive and tender were on solid ground while the rest of the train was perched on the bridge. Having had the earlier experience of two somewhat successful train robberies, Rube reasoned that any of the T&P crew or passengers who might have been inclined to disrupt the robbery would have been placed at a significant disadvantage by being forced to walk down the narrow, precarious trestle.

After the train was stopped, Rube ordered the engineer and fireman to climb down from the cab. At the same time, Jim Burrow, along with another gang member named Bill Brock, rode out of their hiding place in some nearby brush leading two additional horses. Rube instructed the engineer and fireman to negotiate the trestle and accompany him back to the express car. Jim and Brock had gone ahead and positioned themselves near the rear of the car, revolvers at the ready in the event someone might exit the door of the trailing passenger coach.

As with previous train robberies executed by Rube, the express messenger refused to open the locked door. Rube, holding his revolver to the head of the engineer, directed him to return to the engine and retrieve a crowbar. In minutes, the engineer was standing once again beside Rube, who ordered him to pry open the express car door. Once the door was forced open and the messenger saw the gun pointed at the engineer, he raised his hands and offered no resistance.

Rube and Bromley climbed into the express car, forced open the safe, and removed just under $2,000. Moments later, the Burrow brothers, Bromley, and Brock were mounted up and riding away.

At the first opportunity, a posse was formed to pursue the train robbers. Unfortunately, a dense thunderstorm struck the region within minutes after the holdup and the downpour obliterated any tracks that might have been left by the outlaws. Once again, Rube and his gang made an effective escape following a relatively easy robbery.

With his confidence at a renewed high, Burrow lost no time in planning his next train robbery. Three and a half months would pass before his next heist—remarkably the same train at the same place. Before he did that, however, other enterprising train robbers made their marks.

Benbrook, Texas, is the only location in the history of America where the same train was robbed in the same location by the same gang of robbers. Not only that, the same engineer and fireman who were on duty during the first robbery were assigned to the locomotive when the second one took place. Despite the uniqueness of this robbery, details are sketchy and newspaper reports of the time carried scant information about the event. Furthermore, the newspapers did little in the way of follow-up investigation and reporting. In the end, all that was known for certain was that the Rube Burrow gang had struck again.

Repeating the procedure established during the first robbery, Rube and Henderson Bromley scrambled aboard the Texas and Pacific train only a few minutes before it departed the station on September 30, 1887. As before, the two outlaws made their way across the coal tender and arrived at the locomotive cab, where they instructed the engineer to stop the train on the trestle. Recognizing the two robbers, the engineer and fireman seemed to know exactly what they needed to do, offered no resistance, and cooperated as best they could and without saying a word.

Despite the earlier promises by Texas Governor Ross relative to instituting protective measures for the railroads that operated in the Lone Star State, there were no guards, armed or otherwise, on duty on this particular T&P run. With little difficulty, and encountering no resistance whatsoever, Burrow forced the express car door open, climbed in, and holding the express messenger at gunpoint, removed just over $2,700 from the safe. Moments later, the outlaws rode away.

Coincidentally, as with the previous Benbrook train robbery by the Burrow gang, a sudden and violent thunderstorm struck the region and washed away any tracks that might have been left. As a result, the subsequent posses were unable to determine the escape route of the outlaws. Lawmen ranged out in a variety of directions from the robbery site but had no luck in picking up any sign of the bandits.

Following his second Benbrook, Texas, train robbery, Rube Burrow became an oft-hunted man. Wanted posters had been tacked up throughout much of the Lone Star State, and his identity made known to railroad detectives, sheriff departments, local police, and other law enforcement agencies. It is believed by some researchers that he had plans to rob other trains in Texas, but shortly after the September 30 holdup, he felt the pressure of lawmen closing in and decided it was time to lay low.

Eventually Rube decided it was in his best interest to leave Texas all together. He gathered his loot and his gang and made his way back to his childhood home in Lamar County, Alabama, far enough from Texas that he was certain he would not be pursued.

Upon arriving in Alabama, Rube and his gang were taken in by relatives, to whom he presented gifts, all purchased with the money stolen during his Texas train robberies. He, along with brother Jim and associate Bill Brock, were welcomed and assured by these family members that they could hide out for as long as necessary in this sparsely populated northwestern Alabama county.

Wishing to impress those around them, the Burrow gang lived lavishly, and it wasn't long before their money ran out. The easiest way to get more, reasoned Rube, was to do what he felt he did best: Rob another train. After considering a number of options, the outlaws set their sights on a St. Louis, Arkansas, and Texas Railway train two states away at Genoa, Arkansas.

GENOA, ARKANSAS

Toward the end of autumn 1887, Rube Burrow was broke. He summoned his brother Jim and gang member Bill Brock to plan another train robbery. It has bewildered researchers that Rube decided to rob a St. Louis, Arkansas, and Texas train near the tiny town of Genoa, located six miles south of Texarkana, Arkansas, and nearly four hundred miles to the west of Lamar County, Alabama. Researchers concur that he had been convinced his train robbing activities were unknown in Arkansas, and therefore law enforcement authorities would not be alert to any potential robbery scheme.

Rube decided the gang members should employ aliases. On December 3, the Burrow brothers checked into a Texarkana hotel under the names R. Houston and James Buchanan. When Brock arrived, he checked in using his own name, W. L. Brock. His mistake would eventually lead to his arrest.

The three men spent some time observing the schedules of the railroad, then selected December 9 as an ideal date for the robbery. Not wanting to remain in town and generate suspicion, they traveled to Brock's home of Alexander, Texas, located ninety miles southwest of Fort Worth. There, the three men purchased rubber raincoats. They returned to Texarkana by train on the morning of the 9th. From there, they walked the six miles to Genoa, the location they had selected to rob the train. The outlaws had considered renting horses in Texarkana but feared exposing themselves unnecessarily in the town.

That evening as the SLA&T train pulled out of the Genoa station, Rube and Brock climbed to the top of the express car and made their way to the tender. Jim had earlier taken a position farther down the track. As the train was beginning to pick up speed, Rube and Brock made their way across the tender toward the engine. They dropped into the locomotive cab with guns drawn, surprising the engineer and fireman. Rube ordered the engineer to stop the train a short distance ahead.

Once the train had come to a halt, Rube ordered the engineer to unhook the express car from those behind. This done, he had the engineer pull up to a location a few hundred yards ahead where Jim lay in hiding. When the train stopped, the outlaws went to the express car and called for the messenger inside to open it. When he refused, Rube, speaking in a voice loud enough for the messenger to hear, told the engineer to obtain an oilcan and start a fire under the car. Moments later, the messenger opened the door to the express car.

Inside the car, the robbers opened the safe and found $2,000, which they stuffed into sacks. The engineer was then ordered to return to the idling locomotive and continue down the tracks. As the train disappeared around a bend, the robbers began walking northward toward Texarkana. Author Richard Patterson surmised that Rube Burrow presumed the law enforcement authorities would guess that the outlaws rode from the scene on horses. It turned out to be a serious miscalculation; the sheriff at Texarkana, on being apprised of the robbery, quickly formed a posse and headed toward Genoa. The posse rode south along the same track on which the gang was traveling north.[2]

At the last moment, the outlaws heard the oncoming posse and were able to dash into the nearby woods. The lawmen spotted the robbers and opened fire. Fleeing through the cover of forest and undergrowth, the Burrow gang finally reached Texarkana and located a convenient place to hide. As they recovered from their flight, they divided the money from the robbery. This done, the three split up and went in different directions.

Compared to Rube's first four train robberies in Texas, the Genoa holdup was marked by errors. Before fleeing the scene of the crime, the outlaws left two of their rubber slickers, along with a hat, at the scene. Officials of the Southern Express Company contacted the regional office of the Pinkerton National Detective Agency and invited then to participate in the investigation of the case. William McGinn, regarded as one of the agency's top detectives, subsequently arrived in Texarkana.

McGinn noticed that inside the collar of the slickers were the letters "KWP." On the sweatband of the hat was the notation of a hatmaker in Dublin, Texas. McGinn sent another agent to Dublin, who learned that this hat was one of many sold over the course of the year and no specific record of purchasers was kept. The detective also learned that the letters "KWP" found inside the slickers represented a pricing code employed by the seller, located in Alexander, Texas. When questioned, the shopkeeper recalled he had sold the raincoats to a local cowhand named Brock and two of his companions. The descriptions provided by the clerk matched the descriptions of the train robbers. The name "Brock" was checked against registrants at the Texarkana hotel where the name "W. L. Brock" was found.

Additionally the detectives learned that Brock had made two recent trips to Texarkana, and not long after the train robbery, was spotted in Waco, Texas, freely spending a great deal of money. Brock was tracked down and located at his home in Alexander and arrested. He was identified by the engineer of the St. Louis, Arkansas, and Texas train as one of the robbers. A short time later, the authorities convinced Brock that if he cooperated in their investigation, he would be offered a reduced prison sentence. He agreed and named Rube and Jim Burrow as his partners in the holdup.

The two brothers were more difficult to locate and managed to elude pursuit. And while they successfully remained in hiding, Rube began making plans to rob another train. As the Pinkertons were closing in, informants alerted the Burrow gang to their proximity. The detectives hung wanted posters for the outlaws throughout that part of the South. Eluding the Pinkertons only scant hours before they arrived at their hideout, the train robbers escaped on foot. A few days later, they purchased passage on a Louisiana & Nashville train and traveled to Montgomery, Alabama, where they intended to lay low until things cooled down.

The L&N train made several stops along the route. As it made its way toward Montgomery, a sharp-eyed train conductor recognized the Burrow brothers from the wanted posters. At the next stop, he left the train, went to the telegraph office, and alerted officials at the Montgomery station. By the time the train arrived, a squad of lawmen was waiting to apprehend the Burrows.

On being arrested, Rube Burrow argued with the officers that they were victims of a case of mistaken identity, that he and Jim were representatives of a timber company and had arrived in town to conduct business. The police did not fall for the explanation and decided to transport the two men to the police station where they could interrogate them further. Though the two passengers were initially identified as members of the notorious Burrow gang, the lawmen, in a lapse of good judgment, did not search them for weapons. Both were carrying revolvers under their coats.

As the two robbers were being walked into the police station, Rube saw a chance to escape and took it. As the policeman who was escorting him looked away for a moment, Rube turned and made a break for freedom. The officer reached for his revolver, but in the process his coat got caught on a doorknob, distracting him momentarily. By the time the policeman got his weapon out, Rube was long gone.

Jim Burrow was less fortunate. As he attempted to flee, he was immediately tackled and wrestled to the ground and cuffed. He was later sent to Arkansas to stand trial for the Genoa robbery.

As Rube was running away from the police station, he glanced back and spotted a man pursuing him. Believing the pursuer to be a policeman,

Burrow pulled his revolver from beneath his coat, turned, aimed, and fired two shots, each of them striking the man. The chaser stumbled, then fell to the ground, severely wounded and writhing in pain. As it turned out, the victim was not a policeman at all, but a newspaper reporter who was after a story. It took him several weeks to recover.

Rube fled down alleys and between houses and managed to elude his pursuers. He reached the outskirts of town with little difficulty. Spotting the edge of a thick woods one hundred yards beyond, he fled in that direction. Hardened by years of heavy work on his farm, and quite at home in the Alabama woods, Rube had no trouble distancing himself from the lawmen bent on his recapture. He knew how to survive in this kind of environment and was far more comfortable in such surroundings than those who were tracking him. While reports of Rube Burrow sightings arrived at police stations from time to time, and while trackers often came upon recently vacated campsites, the train robber always managed to evade his trackers. In all, Rube succeeded in dodging the law in this manner for two years.

Rube eventually made it back to the friendly environs of Lamar County and his family. Lawmen, however, had been watching the location and soon learned their quarry was in the region. They began closing in again, thus making it difficult for Rube to remain in the area. Realizing it was just a matter of time before he would be apprehended, Rube snuck away from Lamar County. This time, he fled to Florida where he believed he would be safe. In Florida, he worked for a time in the turpentine camps.

While spending an interval in relative safety in the Sunshine State, Rube fell in with a man named Leonard Brock (no relation to gang member Bill). Together, the two men made plans to travel to Arkansas to spring brother Jim from jail. Their plans never materialized. Only a few days before they were to implement them, the men learned that Jim had become ill and died while incarcerated.

Rube decided to return to what he believed he did best—train robbery. He set his sights on holding up an Illinois Central train at Duck Hill, Mississippi.

DUCK HILL, MISSISSIPPI

A few minutes past 10 p.m. on December 15, 1888, Rube Burrow and Leonard Brock sprinted from hiding and raced toward the Illinois Central train as it pulled away from the Duck Hill station. On reaching the tender, they climbed to the top and, on hands and knees, made their way toward the engine where, with revolvers pointed at the engineer and fireman, Burrow ordered the train be halted immediately. The crew was walked back to the express car where Burrow told the messenger to open the door. He did so, and Burrow climbed into the car while Brock held the crew at gunpoint. The safe was opened with no difficulty, and Burrow removed $2,000 in currency, which he began stuffing into a sack.

As Burrow was gathering the bills, the conductor, troubled by the unscheduled halting of the train, suspected the worst. After convincing a passenger, Chester Hughes, to assist him, the conductor secured two rifles, and the two men climbed out of the passenger coach and onto the roof. From their perch, they could see men standing outside the express car and opened fire. Brock responded by getting off several rounds at the attackers. On hearing the fusillade, Burrow, grabbing the sack of money, took a position at the door of the car. Spotting the shooters atop the passenger coach, he fired his weapon several times and managed to hit Hughes with each shot. When the conductor dropped his rifle to assist Hughes, Burrow and Brock made their escape.

BUCKATUNNA, MISSISSIPPI

Rube Burrow made himself scarce for a bit, until he resurfaced on September 25, 1889, almost a year later in Buckatunna, Mississippi, again with Brock and now a new gang member named Rube Smith (also Burrow's cousin). Wearing masks, two of the outlaws climbed onto the baggage blind behind the tender of a Mobile & Ohio train and sneaked forward, dropping into the cab and pointing their revolvers at the engineer, Seak Terrell, and the foreman, Thomas Hurt.

When the train had proceeded two miles south of Buckatunna, Burrow instructed Terrell to stop the train at a certain point on the trestle that bridged the Buckatunna River. The engine, tender, express car, and two mail cars were on the far side of the trestle, with the rest of the train, the passenger coaches, remaining on the span. At this point, the third member of the gang rose out of hiding and joined them. At gunpoint, Terrell and Hurt were herded back to the express car where messenger J. W. Dunning offered no resistance and threw the door open wide.

Burrow instructed Dunning to place the contents of the safe in a canvas bag, $2,700 in all, while Brock and Smith stood guard over the engine crew. Had Burrow spent a bit more time exploring the express car, he might have spotted the $70,000 in brand new currency that had been placed not far from the door. Meanwhile, mail clerk W. C. Bell was troubled by the odd stoppage of the train and suspected a robbery might be taking place. Bell hoisted a number of registered packages, twenty-four in all, and attempted to hide them in the baggage car. Before he could accomplish his plan however, he was intercepted by Burrow, who took possession of the parcels.

The conductor, Billy Scholes, was also concerned. He obtained a lantern and a rifle, climbed out of one of the passenger cars, and was tentatively making his way across the trestle when he was spotted by the robbers. A volley of shots in his direction sent him scurrying back to the coach.

Burrow ordered the engineer and fireman back into the cab and told Terrell to continue on down the track. As the train pulled away, the outlaws faded into the nearby woods. They dusted their trail with red pepper, a procedure employed by outlaws to throw tracking dogs off their scent. While reports differ, most believe the robbers took a total of $5,000 from the express and mail cars.

CENTURY, FLORIDA

Rube Burrow's next, and final, train robbery was undertaken as a solo act. It has never been clear why his gang members were not involved, but on the evening of September 1, 1890, Burrow stopped a Louisville & Nashville train over a trestle spanning the Escambia River in northwestern Florida, near the border with Alabama. The closest town of any significance was Century. After taking money from the express car, Burrow fled.

Law enforcement authorities took up his trail within a short time, but the outlaw managed to stay ahead of pursuit for weeks.

Louisville & Nashville railroad detectives, along with investigators associated with the Southern Express Company, collaborated to put an end to Burrow's train robbing depredations once and for all. Nearly a month following his robbery of the L&N train, Burrow was tracked to the tiny farm community of Repton, Alabama, northeast of Mobile, but he slipped away as the law was closing in. The manhunt continued for another full year, sometimes with the detectives coming within several yards of the train robber, other times with Burrow eluding pursuit and vanishing for days on end.

Finally, on October 7, 1890, Burrow was tracked down to a cabin a short distance west of Myrtleville, Alabama. Lawmen closed in, and with the place surrounded by more than twenty armed law enforcement personnel, Burrow surrendered. He was placed in irons and transported to the nearby county seat at Linden. On arriving, Burrow's captors found the jail locked and the sheriff unavailable. They marched the outlaw to an unoccupied office next door and secured his chains to an iron ring fastened to the floor. Two deputies, John McDuffie and Jesse Hildreth, along with another man, stood guard. Deputy J. D. Carter and a fifth deputy were sleeping in an adjacent building.

During the night, Burrow, who had not eaten for nearly twenty-four hours, complained of hunger and requested that one of the deputies bring him a cloth sack that had been in his possession at the time of capture. The sack, Burrow explained, had some food in it. Deputy McDuffie made a casual inspection of the sack and saw that it contained some ginger snaps. He handed it over to Burrow. A moment later, Burrow pulled a revolver from the sack and pointed it at the surprised, and careless, McDuffie. Not only had McDuffie not detected the heavy revolver in the sack, but he had left his own handgun lying on a table several feet away. Inexplicably, the two other deputies, who by now had awakened, were unarmed.

At gunpoint, Burrow ordered Deputy Hildreth to lead him to Deputy Carter. During the capture of Burrow, Carter had seized the train

THE OLD WEST'S INFAMOUS TRAIN ROBBERS AND THEIR HISTORIC HEISTS

robber's rifle and Burrow wanted it back. On arriving at the building where Carter and the other deputy were sleeping, Burrow instructed Hildreth to call out to him and tell him there was a problem at the jail and that his presence was needed. Burrow then took up a position behind a nearby tree, his revolver at the ready.

When the sleepy Carter walked out of the door strapping on his gun belt, Burrow called out to him and told him he wanted his rifle returned to him. Carter's response was to reach for his revolver. He was not fast enough. Before he could aim his weapon, Burrow shot him in the left shoulder. Undeterred, the plucky Carter got off four rapid shots. With the last one, Burrow was struck. In an odd reaction, the outlaw leaped high into the air, then fell to the ground where he writhed in pain. As witnesses gathered around the wounded man, they watched as Burrow desperately gasped for air. A moment later, he was dead.

On October 9, the train transporting Rube Burrow's body pulled into the Sulligent station in Lamar County. Burrow's family members, who had been informed of his death and alerted to the time of arrival of the body, had gathered. The body of the now famous train robber had been placed in an inexpensive wooden casket. When the train finally came to a stop, the door to the express car slid open. In a deliberate show of contempt for the slain outlaw, a team of Southern Express Company officials who had been placed in charge of the body unceremoniously shoved the casket out of the car, causing it to land heavily onto the station platform. Without a word, the express personnel slammed the car door closed. Moments later, the train, amid a blowing whistle and belching smoke, pulled away from the station.

A train, the object of so many of Rube Burrow's outlaw escapades, had delivered the now famous robber to his final resting place.

With the end of Rube Burrow and the apparent dispersal of what little was left of his gang, railroad officials, particularly those in Texas, felt relief. Finally, the scourge of rail companies was dead and would no longer menace express car shipments.

Their relief, however, was short-lived. Rather than come to an end, the problems with train robbers were about to begin anew. Outlaws like Sam Bass, Rube Burrow, and others had shown like-minded desperadoes how it could be done, and several new enterprising train robbers seized the opportunity.

Bill Whitley

Brack Cornett

5

The Bill Whitley/Brack Cornett Gang

BILL WHITLEY WAS NO STRANGER TO CRIME AND VIOLENCE. BORN WILliam Henry Whitley on September 7, 1864, on a farm in Itawamba County, Mississippi, he was the youngest of several children brought into the world by parents William Taylor Whitley and Elizabeth Henry Whitley. (Some research materials state that Whitley was born in the town of Smithville in Monroe County, Mississippi.)

Bill Whitley's older brothers served in the Confederate Army during the Civil War. Following the conflict, the area around Itawamba County in northeastern Mississippi was characterized as "wild" with rampant and "violent lawlessness."[1] Raids and killings were not an uncommon sight for the young Whitley.

In 1884 one of Whitley's brothers was shot and killed by a lawman. Seeking revenge, and perhaps looking for an outlet for his own explosive nature, Whitley went on a rampage and in the end, was responsible for the killing of eight men. Though his family members insisted his activities were exaggerated, there is no denying the facts.

Though the chronology is unclear, it is known that Whitley migrated to Texas (some say it was in the company of his parents), and for a time lived in Lampasas where he pursued his criminal and brutal ways. There, he also courted and married Cordelia Lucinda Cox. (At least one publication gives her name as Cornelia Cox.) The union created some problems for the Cox family when some were arrested and charged with harboring a criminal.

Bill and Lucinda became the parents of two daughters: Minnie Margaret born in November 1884, and Temperance Alice born in March 1886. In spite of the responsibilities related to supporting a growing family, Whitley continued to pursue his criminal activities. Law enforcement authorities were constantly on his trail even to the point of posting watchmen near his home. Believing he needed to remove himself from the Lampasas area, Whitley decided to leave his wife and children in the care of her brother while he fled to England. A short time later, the brother moved the family to Coryell County, Texas.

When Whitley returned to Texas, he immediately fell in league with a man named Brack Cornett. Braxton "Brack" Cornett was born May 22, 1841, in Clinton County, Missouri, and raised in Goliad County, Texas. (Some accounts list his birthplace as Goliad County.) Little is known of Cornett's life prior to his joining up with Bill Whitley to rob banks and trains. He often went by the alias, "Captain Dick."

Whitley and Cornett put together a gang and became successful bank and train robbers. Law enforcement authorities who pursued the outlaws alternately referred to the robbers as the Bill Whitley Gang and the Brack Cornett Gang.

During the year 1887, Whitley and Cornett, along with a band of ten additional gang members, conducted a series of bank robberies from which they netted several thousand dollars. On February 15, 1888, Whitley, Cornett, and another ten men entered the Bank of Cisco, Texas, minutes before closing time and asked cashier C. C. Leveaux for some change. When Leveaux looked up, he was staring into the barrels of several drawn revolvers. By the time the gang walked out of the bank, they had stolen $9,000 in gold and silver, along with some bank notes. Stories circulated that the loot was buried somewhere near Cisco, but as far as anyone knows, none of it has ever been recovered.

Though Bill Whitley and Brack Cornett were successful bank robbers, their outlaw reputation rests largely on their train robberies.

FLATONIA, TEXAS

In 1887, a band of outlaws took over a Southern Pacific train near Flatonia, Texas, about midway between Houston and San Antonio, and made off with thousands of dollars from the express car as well as a significant amount of loot taken from the passengers. It is believed that some members of the gang had previous train robbery experience, likely having participated in the McNeil heist with Rube Burrow.

Flatonia is located in Fayette County between Houston and San Antonio. As the eastbound Southern Pacific slowly pulled away from the Flatonia station at 12:30 a.m. on the evening of June 18, 1887, two men, apparently emulating the style of Rube Burrow and his gang, climbed aboard the back of the coal tender, made their way across the top of the fuel supply, and dropped down into the locomotive cab. By this time, so common was this boarding technique by train robbers, that it is surprising the railroad companies were unprepared for the tactic. It would have been a simple matter for the railroad company to station armed guards in the cab alongside the engineer and fireman, but no attempt had been made to do so.

At first, the engineer, B. A. Pickens, thought the newcomers were hobos, and he ordered them off the train. In response, the two strangers pulled revolvers and held them to the heads of Pickens and the fireman. Pickens was ordered to keep the train moving at a slow rate of speed until he was instructed otherwise. After the train had traveled about a mile and a half, one of the robbers instructed the engineer to stop the train just across a trestle a short distance ahead and where a large fire could be seen burning next to the track. In the light of the fire, Pickens could see what he later stated were five additional armed men poised to approach the train. Later, others estimated the total number of robbers in waiting numbered at least ten. Parked just beyond the group of men was a wagon pulled by two horses.

When the train first pulled to a stop, the robbers held a short conference. During this time, engineer Pickens managed to slip away and make his way to the first passenger coach. There, he alerted the travelers as to what was about to transpire, warning them to hide as many of their valuables as they could under the seats. Word quickly spread to the other passenger cars. Moments later, the robbers entered the first car, and with swift efficiency walked through the passenger coaches relieving travelers of what money, watches, jewelry, and other items they were unable to conceal.

One of the train robbers, clearly one of the gang leaders, was referred to by his companions as "Captain Dick," Brack Cornett's nickname.

From the time he boarded the train until he rode away with his gang, he constantly sucked on a stick of hard candy.

Seated in one of the passenger cars was a man named Quintas, who was reportedly a high-ranking colonel in the Mexican army. On learning that the train was being robbed, Quintas told his manservant sitting next to him to prepare his revolver. He boasted out loud to all within earshot that he would kill anyone who tried to rob him. By the time the bandits reached Quintas, however, the officer had apparently lost his nerve and was easily disarmed. The outlaw called Captain Dick approached Quintas, told him he did not like Mexicans, and said, "I would just as soon kill you as eat my breakfast."[2] Nervous, the colonel handed over his billfold containing $400.

When the robbers reached the sleeping car, they came upon a passenger who was frantically trying to hide his money under a mattress. He was pulled aside and beaten. A search of his hiding place yielded over $1,000. In another sleeping compartment, two salesmen were held up. When they hesitated after being ordered to turn over their valuables, they, too, were beaten. A female passenger who was likewise slow in turning over her purse was slapped.

When the outlaws had finished with the coaches, they approached the express car several dozen yards away. Inside, Wells, Fargo express messenger Frank Folger, realizing that a robbery was taking place, began stuffing sacks of cash into the stove in the hope the robbers would never think to search there. After forcing their way into the car, however, the bandits spotted Folger in the act of trying to hide the money. Angered, one of them smacked the messenger alongside the head with the butt of his revolver.

When the moneybags had been retrieved from the stove, the robbers turned their attention to the safe, which could be opened only with a key. One of the bandits commented that moments before arriving at the express car he had seen the messenger toss what appeared to be a key out the express car door, and that it had landed on the ground a short distance away. Folger was ordered to step outside the car and locate the key. When he refused, one of the bandits yanked a skinning knife from a belt scabbard and cut slits in both of his ears, with a promise of worse to come if he did not retrieve the key. Folger set about trying to locate the key with no further resistance, and a few moments later handed it over to one of the gang members.

With the same efficiency they manifested from the beginning of the robbery, the outlaws opened the safe, removed the contents, jumped from the car, and ran toward their horses. Moments later they were riding away in different directions.

The total amount of loot taken during the robbery remains unclear. One account states that $600 was removed from the express car and another $1,000 from the passengers. Another report estimated the total haul at more than $3,000.

In a short time, several posses were organized to pursue the train robbers, but success was slow in coming. A man named George Shoaf, a well-known gambler from San Antonio, was arrested and charged with participation in the robbery. Shoaf, however, vehemently denied any role in the event and said he could prove he was not within miles of the holdup, and that he could provide witnesses declaring he was playing poker in San Antonio. His alibi proved to be legitimate.

The robbery of the Southern Pacific train at Flatonia marked a signifi-cant change in the actions of the perpetrators. For the first time, passengers and crew were subjected to harsh, brutal, and, by all accounts, unnecessary treatment by the bandits. Heretofore, passengers and crew were generally left unharmed unless they offered a threat. When news of the event made its way to the papers, the public reacted with anger and demanded that law enforcement authorities move quickly to arrest the gang of robbers. Texas Governor Lawrence S. Ross likewise voiced outrage at the behavior of the train robbers and vowed to have them captured. Likely bending to the will of the powerful railroads, Ross announced that from that day on, "five to ten well-armed fighting men"[3] would be assigned to each train moving through the state of Texas. To accomplish this, Ross com-missioned 390 new Texas Rangers. Despite Governor Ross's bombastic proclamations, train robbery in Texas slowed down not one bit.

Newspapers reported that Wells, Fargo, the company in charge of the express car that was robbed, offered a $1,000 reward for the "capture and conviction"[4] of each of the robbers. Following this announcement, Gover-nor Ross lost no time in adding $500 to that amount, along with a promise that the robbers would be caught. In addition, the Southern Pacific Company contributed $250, and the US government kicked in another $200. In all, a total amount of $1,950 for the capture and conviction of each of the robbers was being dangled in front of the public in the hope that one or more citizens might come forth with information. It didn't take long.

After reading an article about the Flatonia train robbery, a Giddings, Texas, resident named Mike Buck revealed that the leader of the gang was his great-great grandfather Bill Whitley. Though it seemed unlikely that such a generational gap could occur, especially since Whitley was only twenty-three years old, it was determined that Buck and Whitley were, in fact, close relatives. Buck said it was Whitley and another man named Brack Cornett who had boarded the train at Flatonia and forced the engineer to pull it to a stop. Buck related that Whitley had also been involved in the McNeil train robbery one month earlier. Whitley, known throughout this area of Texas as an unsavory character, had also robbed the First National Bank at Cisco, Texas.

The search for the Flatonia train robbers involved law enforcement authorities from the state of Texas, sheriff departments from the surrounding counties, Wells, Fargo detectives, and local police officers, as well as citizens. The state of Texas, along with the US government, placed significant pressure on lawmen to bring the bandits to justice, and provided a contingent of US marshals to assist in the pursuit.

Weeks passed, but lawmen remained hard on the trail of the train robbers. In September two men—Tom Jones and Jim Henson—were found and arrested in San Saba County for "illicit dealings in horse flesh."[5] While in custody, Jones bragged about his role in the Flatonia train robbery to another prisoner. Soon afterward, his jailers determined that Jones had indeed been part of the gang of bandits. Henson, as it turned out, was involved not only with the Flatonia robbery but also with the McNeil train robbery only two months earlier.

Henson, who had turned state's evidence related to a number of stagecoach robberies, was charged with complicity in the Flatonia robbery by San Saba Sheriff Metcalf. Henson agreed to reveal the names of the gang members as well as provide evidence to convict them on the condition that he be released. A judge would not agree to such a condition, but did promise a lighter sentence in return for his cooperation. With information provided by Henson, another of the gang members—John Criswell—was arrested several days later. More arrests followed.

At 10 a.m. on September 27, a number of the train robbers, shackled and chained, were arraigned before US Commissioner Ruggles and District Attorney Kelborg, who represented the United States. Though newspaper reports differ on the names of the robbers who appeared in court, it is likely the list included Tom Jones, Jim Henson, John Criswell, Ed Reaves (alias Pat Reaves), J. A. "Bud" Powell (alias Charles Thompson), and a man named Humphries. The robbers remaining at large included Whitley, Brack Cornett (alias Captain Dick), John Hill, and John Barbour.

In the courtroom, the gang member identified as Humphries, hoping to escape a prison sentence, explained in detail how the entire Flatonia train robbery was planned and executed. He claimed he had no part in the robbery other than driving a wagon and was not involved with taking anyone's money. During his testimony, Humphries referred to the Flatonia train robbers as the Bill Whitley Gang. Of the men appearing in court, only J. A. Powell and Ed Reaves were made to stand trial. They were found guilty and sent to prison.

The remaining members of the gang who were still on the run—Whitley, Cornett, Hill, and Barbour—evaded capture and went on to attempt another train robbery, this one at Harwood, Texas.

HARWOOD, TEXAS

For the previous ten years, train robbery momentum had been building in Texas, slowly but most certainly. In the cases of Sam Bass and Rube Burrow, multiple robberies were planned and executed by the same persons and their same partners over and over. On the other hand, the Bill Whitley Gang, which had been involved in the train robberies at Flatonia and McNeil, had experienced some successes despite the fact that half the gang had been arrested, and some had been tried, convicted, and sent to prison.

Though an experienced and successful train robber, as well as a bonafide bad man, Bill Whitley never received the recognition or notoriety of Sam Bass or Reuben Burrow, although he was just as active and efficient.

While he was still on the run from the law for his involvement with the Flatonia and McNeil robberies, the bold and daring Whitley decided to undertake yet another holdup. This one proved to be his undoing.

Whitley decided to rob the Southern Pacific train at Harwood, Texas, on September 22, 1888. Harwood was a small town located in Gonzalez County. For the job, Whitley relied on assistance from Braxton "Brack" Cornett. (Some researchers believe it was Cornett's idea to rob the train and that he enlisted Whitley to assist him.)

Somehow, rumor of a potential robbery of the SP train began to spread, and word eventually reached US Marshal John Rankin. Assuming his information was accurate, Rankin decided to thwart the bandits by hiding on the train and surprising them when they arrived. Rankin recruited Deputy Duval West, along with a number of Texas Rangers. After arming themselves, and packing extra ammunition, they boarded the train on the appointed day and seated themselves in a passenger car.

After the last passenger was aboard and the express and mail cars secured, the train pulled away from the station amid a loud whistle and a belching of black smoke from the locomotive. After traveling about three miles and picking up speed, the train was stopped by a gang of three robbers. As Bill Whitley, Brack Cornett, and the third outlaw whose identity remains unknown, approached the passenger car, the lawmen opened fire, scattering the outlaws and ultimately driving them away.

In addition to thwarting the train robbery, the aggressive tactic employed by the lawmen was sufficient to send Whitley and Cornett into escape mode. Certain that a posse would not be long in tracking them, the three outlaws rode away from the robbery site as fast as possible. This time luck was not with them, for the determined lawmen did indeed pursue them with the intent of not giving up until they captured or killed the train robbers.

Following the botched robbery attempt on the Southern Pacific train at Harwood, Texas, and in addition to the lawmen tracking them from the train, a posse was formed. It immediately went in pursuit of the would-be robbers. For three days, the lawmen, composed primarily of US marshals, followed the tracks of the outlaws and finally caught up with and encountered them in Floresville, Texas, thirty-five miles southeast of San Antonio. While details are sketchy, it is known that when the marshals came upon the train robbers, a shootout took place. Whitley was killed at the onset of the skirmish, and the unidentified gang member arrested. Seeing an opportunity to evade the lawmen, Cornett escaped on horseback.

Whitley was buried in the Mahomet Cemetery in Burnet County, Texas. According to extant documents, he was only twenty-four years old. His headstone reads "He was a kind and affectionate husband, a fond father, and a friend to all." Undoubtedly, some of Whitley's victims would disagree with the inscription.

Texas lawmen took up the chase after Cornett. There exist three widely differing versions of how Cornett met his end. One version has him being overtaken by the pursuing posse and, following a brief gun battle, shot dead.

A second, and more likely, version has Cornett arriving at the ranch of a friend in La Salle County in south Texas. The friend, Alfred Allee, had learned of the recent attempt on the Southern Pacific train at Harwood and was aware that Cornett was involved. He was also aware that Cornett had participated in earlier train robberies. Allee, who was also alleged to be a Texas Ranger, regarded Cornett as dangerous and untrustworthy.

As Cornett rode up to the ranch house early one morning, Allee, who was eating breakfast, looked out the window and spotted him. After strapping on his gun belt and checking the loads in his revolver, the rancher went outside to meet him. As Cornett dismounted from his horse, Allee calmly walked up and shot him, killing him instantly.

Yet a third version of the killing of Cornett made the rounds. It has Allee, in the capacity of Texas Ranger, pursuing the outlaw across three states to a location identified as Frio, Arizona. After Allee caught up with the train robber, a brief shootout occurred, with Cornett being killed.

Evidence for one of the two latter versions being accurate is related to the fact that rancher/ranger Allee received $3,800 in reward money for the killing of Cornett.

With the deaths of Bill Whitley and Brack Cornett, the train robbery gang was now leaderless. The remaining members, on learning of the demise of their compatriots, separated and went their own ways, and were never heard from again.

6

Burt Alvord

BURT ALVORD IS THE MOST FAMOUS TRAIN ROBBER EVER PRODUCED BY the state of Arizona. At various times during his residency there, he pursued careers in law enforcement as well as outlawry. As a lawman, Alvord gained a reputation as a tough, determined, devious, and dangerous man. As an outlaw, he lacked the charm, charisma, and loyalty manifested by other bad men such as Jesse James, Butch Cassidy, and other noted train robbers, and as a result garnered few newspaper headlines outside of Arizona and precious little attention over the years from outlaw historians and enthusiasts.

This cunning train robber was born Albert W. Alvord to Charles E. and Lucy Alvord in Plumas County, California, on September 11, 1867. Father Charles, originally from New York, arrived in California to prospect for gold and held high hopes of becoming wealthy. Though he put in long hours and worked as hard as any man, he had little success. Realizing he was not cut out to be a gold miner, Charles Alvord sought and found steady employment as a mechanic for several mining companies. In time, he ran for public offices and was elected constable and justice of the peace in the various towns and communities where he resided. In 1879 the Alvord family left California and moved to Pima County, Arizona. Following a short stay there, they relocated to the mining town of Tombstone in Cochise County, Arizona.

Young Burt Alvord had little to no formal education, but he watched and learned much from his father's handling of cases as a constable and

Burt Alvord

justice of the peace. As he grew into manhood, Alvord developed a fondness for alcohol and was frequently seen drinking in saloons. He also had a penchant for fisticuffs, was known to never back down, and often went looking for fights. In 1886 Cochise County Sheriff John Slaughter hired nineteen-year-old Burt Alvord as a deputy, despite his somewhat reckless lifestyle and negative reputation. During this period, Alvord was described as intemperate, narrow-minded, and selfish. He gained valuable lawman experience, however, as he assisted Slaughter in capturing or killing several cattle rustlers and other bad men during the three years he served as a deputy.

While a deputy, Alvord was unable to refrain from spending a considerable amount of time in saloons drinking, gambling, and fighting. Such activities generated a damaging image of the sheriff's department and gave Slaughter ample reason to reprimand him. Insulted and angered at the rebuke, Alvord quit. Over the next several months he went on to find employment as a lawman in other Arizona towns, including Fairbank and Pearce. In 1896, he met and married Lola Ochoa. A short time later he purchased a ranch and appeared ready and eager to settle down and pursue life as a cattle rancher, while working part time as a deputy.

Two years following his marriage, Alvord's father died. It is unclear what effect this had on him, but he immediately resigned his position as deputy, left his wife and ranch, and entered into a life of crime. Within weeks, Alvord undertook a search for and found Billy Stiles and "Three Fingered Jack" Dunlop, two noted outlaws he had once pursued as a lawman. With Stiles and Dunlop, along with others, Alvord formed a gang and immediately set about committing armed robberies throughout Cochise County.

Alvord and Stiles were captured following a robbery but escaped. Dissatisfied with the small amount of money acquired from robbing travelers and stores, Alvord began to set his sights on richer targets. After casting about, he decided that the big money could be had from robbing trains. He began to formulate plans and soon decided on a target—a Southern Pacific train that stopped at Cochise Junction.

COCHISE JUNCTION, ARIZONA

In 1899 Cochise Junction in southwestern Arizona's Cochise County was a brief stop on the Southern Pacific Railroad line. Here, trains took on coal and water. Located ten miles southwest of Willcox, Cochise Junction, now simply called Cochise, boasted a population of three thousand people. Today less than fifty people reside in the community. Though virtually unknown to most residents of Arizona today, this seemingly insignificant railroad stop was the site of a daring train robbery that involved the sheriff of Willcox, as well as three additional well-known residents of the town.

During the night of September 11, 1899, as a westbound Southern Pacific train was taking on water at Cochise Junction, two men hiding behind the small wooden station donned masks, approached the engine, and climbed aboard. At gunpoint, they ordered the engineer and fireman to uncouple the far end of the Wells, Fargo express car from the rest of the train. The express car was located behind the coal tender that was directly behind the engine. This done, the bandits instructed the engineer to pull the shortened train forward approximately one mile before stopping. Once the train was halted, the two men forced open the door to the express car and climbed inside.

While one of the outlaws stood guard over the frightened express messenger, the other tied several sticks of dynamite to a large iron safe. After lighting the fuse, the outlaws and the messenger climbed out of the car. Moments later the explosion had blown the door completely off the safe. Climbing back inside the express car, the robbers gathered up $30,000 worth of recently minted and uncirculated gold coins and placed them into two canvas bags. Leaving the express car, the robbers carried the sacks to their horses, tied them on, and rode away into the night. While terrified and intimidated, neither the engineer, fireman, nor express car messenger were harmed.

Once the train robbers were out of sight, the engineer backed the locomotive to Cochise Junction and recoupled it to the passenger coaches. As he did so, the fireman ran into the station to telegraph law enforcement authorities but found the wires had been cut. A few more minutes passed before they located a nearby resident who agreed to ride to Willcox to inform the sheriff of the robbery.

Burt Alvord has been identified, by at least one writer, as the sheriff of Willcox at the time. Other references refer to him as a deputy sheriff, and still others identify him as a constable. Whatever his law enforcement–related position, Alvord, on being informed of the train robbery, lost no time in forming a posse. On arriving at the scene of the robbery, however, Alvord, in spite of objections from others, determined the train robbers had left no tracks and that he was unable to pursue.

Within a few weeks of the robbery of the Southern Pacific train, the incident being, for the most part, forgotten by area residents, a significant development occurred. An uncirculated gold coin was used to purchase drinks at a Willcox saloon. A sharp-eyed bartender noticed the coin and, believing it was related to the recent train robbery, alerted Wells, Fargo detectives, as well as the Arizona Rangers. The coin was subsequently identified as being part of the stolen loot.

The detectives and Rangers moved through town asking questions and soon identified the man who passed the coin. Eyewitnesses came forth and identified a local barfly and ne'er-do-well named Bob Downing as the man who passed the coin. Downing, however, denied any knowledge of the incident and provided the alibi that he had been playing poker with Burt Alvord during the night of the train robbery. It is believed that Downing once rode with noted Texas train robber Sam Bass. Initially, it appeared that Downing had an airtight alibi, but Ranger Burt Grover remained suspicious and decided to probe further.

Grover learned that the poker game had taken place in Schweitzer's Saloon. In addition to Downing and Alvord, two others were involved: Matt Burts and Billy Stiles. Downing, Burts, and Stiles occasionally were employed as deputies and sometimes served as Alvord's bodyguards. Willcox residents regarded all three men as thugs and bullies, and they were to be avoided at all costs.

Ranger Grover harbored suspicions of all four of the poker players. After studying them for a time, he identified Stiles as the weakest of the quartet and decided to concentrate his efforts on him. Pulling Stiles aside one evening, Grover told him he knew that he and his friends were involved in the robbery of the Southern Pacific train and that he had learned that Alvord and Downing were planning on blaming the crime on him. After placing Stiles under arrest, Grover told him his companions planned on killing him. Frightened, Stiles confessed and explained how the robbery and the alibi had been arranged. On the night of the poker game, according to Stiles, he and Burts slipped out the back door of Schweitzer's Saloon, robbed the train, and returned. The only person who saw the two men leave the game was a waiter who was subsequently bribed or threatened by Alvord.

Ranger Grover met with the other law enforcement authorities as well as the Wells, Fargo detectives, and plans were made to arrest the other three men. Burts departed Willcox before he could be apprehended but Downing and Alvord were placed under arrest and transported to the jail in Tombstone. By this time, Stiles realized he had been duped and grew resistant to the authorities. He refused to sign a confession and informed the lawmen he would not testify against Alvord and Downing.

Grover had another idea. He arranged to have Downing released and planned to have him followed to see if he would lead authorities to the rest of the loot. Suspicious, Downing did no such thing. Alvord remained in jail where Wells, Fargo detectives interrogated him and promised a light sentence if he would tell them where the gold coins were hidden. The same offer was made to Stiles. Stiles led the detectives to believe that he would cooperate but wanted to think about the offer for a few days.

Stiles had other plans in mind. On April 8, 1900, he and Alvord escaped from the Tombstone jail. In the process, twenty-four other prisoners were freed. Over the next several weeks, Alvord and Stiles rode throughout Cochise County stealing cattle and committing robberies. And wasting little time, they made plans to undertake another train robbery.

The robbery of the Southern Pacific train near Cochise Junction was the last reported successful train holdup in Arizona.

FAIRBANK, ARIZONA

Today, Fairbank is a ghost town located near the San Pedro River fifteen miles northeast of Sierra Vista. Named for railroad financier Nathaniel

Kellogg Fairbank, the town was established in 1881. It was the rail stop nearest to the town of Tombstone and for a time was regarded as important in the development of southeastern Arizona. In addition, the town of Fairbank served as an important supply point for the numerous freighters hauling ore from the mines at Tombstone to the mills at Contention City and Charleston. For a time, the town boasted a population of one hundred residents, a Wells, Fargo office, a meat market, a mercantile, and a stage station.

On February 15, 1900, Fairbank was the site of an unusual train robbery attempt. On this evening, the Southern Pacific train pulled into the station as part of its normal stop on the Benson-Nogales run. Passengers were allowed to disembark and mill around the station platform smoking and visiting while packages from the express car were unloaded.

Suddenly, five men intent on robbing the express car appeared on the platform among the passengers. Most researchers are convinced that the leader of the gang was Burt Alvord, and that he was accompanied by "Three Fingered Jack" Dunlop, Bravo Juan Yoas, Billy Stiles, Bob Brown, and two brothers named Owen. Both Alvord and Stiles had been lawmen in Cochise County. Working as the express car messenger on this night was Jeff Milton. Milton had agreed to substitute for another agent who was too sick to make the run.

By this time in 1900, Milton had experienced many adventures, most of them relating to working as a lawman. At fifteen, he lied about his age and enlisted in the Texas Rangers. After serving four years, he traveled to New Mexico and found work as a US Deputy Marshal. For a time during the 1880s, he served as a deputy under Cochise County Sheriff John Slaughter. During this period, Milton became a veteran of several manhunts and shootouts. Later, Milton served as Chief of Police in El Paso, Texas.

From the express car, Milton heard someone from the platform shout "Hands up!" Initially, Milton thought a joke was being played on him. A moment later someone approached the car and yelled for him to raise his hands and come out. A second later a shot was fired, the bullet knocking the hat from Milton's head. Milton reached for his revolver but suddenly remembered he had left it on a table deep inside the car. Near the door where he stood, however, leaned a sawed-off shotgun. Milton was tempted to grab it and return fire but was afraid of hitting some of the passengers.

Another shot from one of the robbers struck Milton in the left arm, shattering the bone. In pain, he dropped to the floor of the car. One of the bandits, believing the messenger was dead, approached the door. On his back, Milton reached for the shotgun. When the outlaws climbed inside the car, he fired. Dunlop was struck with eleven shotgun pellets. Another pellet struck Yoas who had come alongside his companion. Dunlop fell to the floor of the car, writhing in pain. Complaining that he had been wounded, Yoas, bleeding, jumped from the car and ran toward his horse.

Milton was bleeding badly from the wound to his arm, which had severed an artery. Desperate, he improvised a tourniquet that managed to inhibit the loss of blood somewhat. After fastening the tourniquet, Milton pulled the keys to the express car safe from his pocket and tossed them into a pile of packages located at the far end of the car. He laid down on the floor of the car and pretended to be dead.

A moment later, Alvord and the rest of the bandits climbed into the car. Milton's pockets were searched for the key to the safe but nothing was found. As Alvord was preparing to shoot Milton again, the train's engineer arrived and intervened, arguing that Milton was already dead. The bandits inspected the safe and quickly realized they would not be able to open it without a key. Angered they fired several rounds from their rifles at the walls and ceiling of the express car. Having vented their frustration, they picked up the badly wounded Dunlop and made their way out of the car, off the platform, and to their horses that were tied up a short distance away.

Milton, no stranger to shootouts, thwarted the train robbery attempt, but for the moment his own life was in danger as he continued to bleed out. He was tended to by crewmen and passengers who finally succeeded in stifling the blood loss. The railroad dispatched a special engine and boxcar to carry the now weakened and delirious express car messenger to the hospital at Tucson. On Milton's arrival, Dr. H. W. Fenner tied the shattered bone together with piano wire. Two days later when it became apparent that this method was insufficient, Milton was transported to San Francisco, California, where he was examined at the Southern Pacific Hospital. The doctors agreed that the arm needed to be amputated, but Milton refused. He enlisted a friend to take him to the office of Dr. George E. Goodfellow, across town. Goodfellow cleaned out the wound and patched the arm back together, but informed Milton that the limb would be useless for the rest of his life. The physician was correct; Milton was never able to use the disabled arm. Following the treatment provided by Goodfellow, Milton's left arm ended up two to three inches shorter than the right. Unable to work as an express car messenger, Milton retired to Tombstone, Arizona. For a time he worked for the US Immigration Service as a border rider. Later, Milton moved to Tucson where he lived for the remainder of his life. He died on May 7, 1947, at the age of eighty-five.

"Three Fingered Jack" Dunlop never recovered from the shotgun blast he received from Milton. Several days following the attempted robbery at Fairbank, the outlaw died from his wounds.

After escaping from the Fairbank train robbery debacle, Burt Alvord went into hiding for a time. Late in 1900, he was captured, taken to Tombstone, and placed in the town jail. Learning that his old friend was locked up, Billy Stiles rode to Tombstone, observed the comings and goings at the jail, and when he thought the time was right, he broke Alvord out. In the process, a deputy was wounded, and Stiles released another twenty-four prisoners. Alvord went into hiding and was not heard from for the next two years.

In 1902, in exchange for a reduced sentence and a share of the reward money, Alvord surrendered to the Arizona Rangers to assist them in the pursuit and capture of Mexican bandit Augustine Chacon. Chacon was caught, tried, convicted, and hung. When it came time for Alvord to serve his sentence, he regretted making the promise and escaped again, once more in the company of Billy Stiles. The two men returned to their criminal ways throughout southeastern Arizona and were, ironically, pursued by the same Arizona Rangers Alvord had previously assisted.

The two outlaws were recaptured in 1903 but escaped a short time later. Alvord, eager to end the hunt for him, sent the bodies of two dead Mexicans to Tombstone with a note indicating they were Alvord and

Stiles. The ruse was quickly discovered, and pursuit of Alvord and Stiles was resumed with renewed enthusiasm. The two men were tracked to the northeastern Sonoran border town of Naco in February 1904. A shootout ensued with Alvord and Stiles suffering wounds. Outnumbered and outgunned, they surrendered.

Alvord was sentenced to two years in the Yuma prison, which he served. After he was released, he traveled to Central America. The last record of his activities there indicated he had found employment working on the Panama Canal. Following that, no account of his whereabouts has ever been found. Alvord simply disappeared and was never heard from again. Alvord Road in Tucson was named after the former lawman and outlaw.

Fairbank, Arizona, ceased to be an important train and freight wagon stop when the silver mines around Tombstone played out. A short time later, the town was abandoned. Today, it is listed on the official Ghost Town Trails and Tombstone Territory Map of Cochise County.

7

Butch Cassidy and the Sundance Kid

THE TWO OUTLAWS—BUTCH CASSIDY AND THE SUNDANCE KID—ARE inextricably linked, largely due to the 1969 western movie of the same name, as well as subsequent print and film treatments. The two outlaws are often represented as boon companions robbing banks and trains together throughout their outlaw careers in both the United States and South America. Much of this is not true.

Cassidy and the Sundance Kid embarked on their outlaw careers separately and in widely separated locations, coming together only during the latter stages of their exploits in the United States and South America. While Cassidy holds the strongest reputation as a train robber, the truth is, the Sundance Kid robbed his first train seven years before Cassidy robbed his. For the better part of Cassidy's outlaw career, the Sundance Kid was a relative latecomer to the gang. Most of the time, Cassidy's more or less constant companion was a fellow outlaw named Elzy Lay. The Sundance Kid and Cassidy were involved in several holdups and did travel to South America together, along with a woman, Etta Place.

The Sundance Kid, whose real name was Harry Alonzo Longabaugh, was born near Phoenixville, Pennsylvania, in 1867, the last of five children of Josiah Long-abaugh and Annie Place. Phoenixville is located a few miles northwest of Philadelphia. The original spelling of the family surname name was Langenbach.

The Sundance Kid

Butch Cassidy

Most accounts of Harry's youth portray him as unsettled and unstable. He was particularly close to his sister, Samanna, and he often found refuge in reading books. When he was thirteen years old, Harry went to live with the Wilmer Ralston family in West Vincent, Pennsylvania, ten miles from Phoenixville. Though technically in the employ of Ralston, Harry was little more than an indentured servant. Shortly after turning fourteen, Harry left the Ralston household and drifted on his own from one job to another.

During his travels, Harry discovered dime novels, and whenever he had any spare change he would purchase them. He was particularly infatuated with the adventures and escapades associated with the desperadoes and outlaws of America's Wild West. Likely as a result of being influenced by the novels, Harry purchased a revolver and taught himself to shoot, eventually becoming quite skilled with the weapon.

When he was fifteen years old, Harry moved to Illinois to live with cousins. The relatives perceived greater opportunities for making a living in the West, so they sold the Illinois farm and moved to Durango, Colorado. Cousin George raised horses and employed Harry to break and train them. Two years later, they all moved to Cortez, Colorado. Harry continued to break horses for George in addition to working on a neighboring ranch. In time, he grew to be a proficient horseman. During this time, Harry encountered men who would eventually play a major role in his life. They included Butch Cassidy, Matt Warner, Dan Parker, and others. In 1886, Harry traveled to Montana and secured a job on the N Bar N Ranch near Miles City. He was nineteen years old. Here, he met Wild Bunch member Harvey "Kid Curry" Logan.

Leaving his job at the N Bar N, Harry traveled to Wyoming in search of work and arrived at the VVV Ranch near the town of Sundance. The winter of 1886–1887 was the worst in the history of the state of Wyoming. As a result, hundreds of head of cattle were frozen to death and cowhands laid off. With no prospects for a job and no money in his pockets, Harry stole a horse, a saddle, a pair of chaps, and a revolver from two cowhands on February 27, 1887, and fled back to Miles City. Before he could affect a complete escape, the now twenty-year-old Longabaugh was overtaken and arrested by Crook County Sheriff James Ryan on

April 8. Locked in handcuffs and leg irons, Harry was placed aboard a train to be returned to Sundance. During the journey, Harry slipped out of his shackles and escaped by leaping from the moving train.

Oddly, Harry made his way back to Miles City. Along the way, he stole seven horses and sold them in the small town of Benton, Montana. In June, Harry was located by Crook County Deputy Sheriff E. K. Davis and stock inspector W. Smith and arrested. He was once again shackled and chained, and transported to the Sundance jail. In Sundance, he was tried for horse theft, found guilty, and sentenced to eighteen months of hard labor. While in jail, according to some writers, Harry acquired the nickname by which he was known for the rest of his life—the Sundance Kid. Others have suggested that a fellow Wild Bunch companion bestowed the nickname on him after he was released from prison. By then, he was twenty-two years of age.

In search of work, Harry traveled to Deadwood, South Dakota, but had little luck in landing a job. Deadwood, a bustling mining town, was filled with saloons and gambling houses, and it was here, according to writers, that Harry learned the finer points of playing cards. It was also here that he took up with some outlaws, which resulted in a few troubles, including seeing his friend Bob Minor shot dead by lawmen. Fearing for his own safety, Harry departed Deadwood and traveled to Cortez, Colorado, and returned to working with his cousin George breaking horses.

After several weeks of working on the ranch, Harry took up with Butch Cassidy, Matt Warner, and Tom McCarty. Though evidence is hard to come by, it is believed by many that Harry was involved in the robbery of the San Miguel Valley Bank in Telluride, Colorado, with Butch Cassidy. On his own again, Harry later returned to Montana and worked on ranches for a time. He also ventured into Alberta, Canada, where he broke and trained horses for the H2 Ranch near Fort Macleod. Some researchers are convinced he also found employment for a time with the Calgary and Edmonton Railway.

By autumn 1881, Harry had returned to Montana. Broke, and with no prospects for work, he decided to rob a train, recruiting two men to assist him: Harry Bass (no relation to Sam Bass) and Bill Madden. Harry set his sights on the Great Northern No. 23 train, with the location of the robbery to be near the small Montana town of Malta.

MALTA, MONTANA

In 1892, Malta, Montana, was a somewhat remote and isolated stop for the Great Northern Railroad along its run from St. Paul, Minnesota, to Butte, Montana. It served primarily as a cattle-shipping depot. Located less than forty-five miles from the Canadian border, Malta was granted its name during an application for a post office in 1890. When asked to come up with a name for what, at the time, was little more than a rail siding, one of the residents spun a globe and when it stopped, he closed his eyes and stabbed his finger at a location. It was the island of Malta in the Mediterranean Sea.

Malta could be considered an ideal setting for a train robbery in 1892. The location was far from any town of significant size, and its population so small that there was little need for lawmen. This may have been a principal reason why the three men were intent on robbing the Great Northern Railroad train No. 23 at that station.

After dropping off a small amount of freight and mail at the Malta station on November 27, the engineer signaled departure and a moment later pulled away. (One account states that the robbery took place on September 29). As the train was picking up speed, none of the town's few residents were about. Suddenly, three men ran out of hiding and jumped aboard the blind between the tender and the express car. They were later identified as Harry Bass, Bill Madden, and Harry Longabaugh, aka the Sundance Kid. About one-half mile from the station, the engineer was surprised when he heard a command from behind. He turned to find himself staring at a masked man pointing a revolver at him. Without wasting words, the intruder ordered the engineer to stop the train.

When the locomotive finally pulled to a halt, the masked stranger instructed the engineer and fireman to climb out of the cab and lead the way back to the express car where they were met by the other two robbers. One of the bandits knocked on the door of the express car and told the messenger inside to open up. At first the messenger, Jerry Hauert, was inclined to resist, but the menacing tone of the outlaw discouraged him.

A moment later he slid the door open, and the robber climbed inside, soon followed by the others. Once in the car, one of the outlaws told Hauert they had no intention of harming him and that they were only interested in any valuables that might reside within.

When they spotted the local safe, the robbers ordered Hauert to open it. When he did, the outlaws were discouraged to find only $20. (One report states the bandits took two checks totaling $53.08, along with two packages valued at less than $11.) A moment later, they found the express safe, and once again commanded Hauert to open it. The frightened messenger explained that he was unable to do so, that the safe could only be opened by express company agents stationed at St. Paul and Butte. They alone, said Hauert, knew the combination. The bandits accepted his explanation.

After rummaging through some of the packages in the express car and finding nothing of value, the robbers, discouraged at the small yield given their effort and risk, told the engineer and fireman to return to the locomotive. During the holdup, the masks of the outlaws kept falling away from their faces and the messenger and engineer got good looks at them. Apparently deciding not to rob the passengers in the trailing coaches, the outlaws jumped from the express car and ran off into the dark. The train proceeded on to the next station where the conductor telegraphed law enforcement authorities and explained the particulars of the robbery. The outlaws, as it turned out, returned to Malta.

Great Northern Railroad executive, J. A. Mayer, immediately offered a reward of $500 for the capture of each of the outlaws. The governor of Montana agreed to match that amount. The rewards amounted to considerably more than what the robbers had stolen, but the railroad company was intent on sending the message that they would not tolerate train robbery.

Sheriff B. F. O'Neal of Choteau County organized and led a posse to search for the robbers. The group arrived in Malta on December 1 and decided to stop at the local tavern for a few drinks before setting out for the scene of the robbery. In the same saloon were three strangers seated at a table near the back of the building, the very quarry the lawmen were pursuing—Harry Bass, Bill Madden, and Harry Longabaugh. On spotting the lawmen, the three outlaws brought forth revolvers and rifles, threatened the posse members, and chased them away.

The train robbers decided it was time to leave town and began making preparations to do so. Unfortunately, they did not leave soon enough. Dogged railroad detective W. Ed Black located and arrested Bass and a companion named William Hunt a short time later. Around the same time, Sheriff O'Neal, along with Cascade County Sheriff Hamilton, arrested Harry Longabaugh as he was boarding an eastbound train preparing to depart Malta. Madden could not be located.

Longabaugh and Bass, along with Hunt and another prisoner, were taken to Helena where they were identified by the conductor of the Great Northern train No. 23 as two of the train robbers. Longabaugh gave his name as J. E. Ebaugh and stated that he sometimes used the alias J. E. Thibado. The prisoners were bound over for trial. Bail was set at $300 for each man, but neither of them had enough money. Two days later, Bill Madden was captured, arrested, and transported to Fort Benton where he was placed in jail to await his trail. While in jail and under questioning, Madden admitted his part in the train robbery and identified his partners as a man named Bass and another named "Loungbo."

The well-attended trial for Bass and Longabaugh was held in Great Falls, Montana. The recommendation was made that "the prisoners be discharged for the reason that nothing has been adduced to show that they were guilty of the charge proffered against them."[1] The case presented by the prosecution deteriorated and the prisoners were released. As Bass was leaving the courthouse, he was immediately re-arrested on charges of burglary based on statements made by Madden. Harry Longabaugh, the Sundance Kid, was allowed to leave town. Because he was using aliases, the prosecution was unaware of the fact that he was the "Longbo" identified by Madden.

Bass and Madden were retried and convicted under the odd and rare charge of "burglary in the night time" in connection with the Malta train robbery. On Christmas morning 1892, they were both admitted to the state penitentiary in Deer Lodge, Montana. Bass eventually received a pardon in January 1897, and after leaving the prison, disappeared from the historical record. Madden was released in January 1898. He moved to Oregon City, Oregon, where he lived out the remainder of his life.

Harry Longabaugh was never recaptured and never faced trial for the Malta train robbery. A few weeks after he was allowed to walk out of the Great Falls courthouse, he found work on a ranch near Culberson, Montana. Among the ranch hands he worked with was Harvey "Kid Curry" Logan. In time, the two men became friends and served as members of the Wild Bunch, noted train robbers led by Butch Cassidy.

The noted American outlaw known as Butch Cassidy was born Robert Leroy Parker on April 13, 1866, in Beaver, Utah, the first of thirteen children. (At least one account claims fourteen children.) Born into a loving and devoted Mormon family, he was raised to be loyal and honest.

Robert's father, Maximillian Parker, purchased 160 acres in Circle Valley, Utah, a broad flat plain surrounded by mountains. The fertile land, believed Parker, would be perfect for growing crops and raising cattle. Importantly for Parker, it looked like a fine place to raise a family. Parker moved his wife and six children into a two-room log cabin in 1879. Robert was thirteen years old.

During the first year on his new property, Maximillian Parker cleared the land, dug irrigation canals, and planted crops. His first harvest was successful. Over the next few years, Parker's cattle herd survived one of the coldest winters in Utah history. He also homesteaded additional property and added more land to his holdings. To make ends meet, Parker found work cutting mine timbers at a small mining town named Frisco. He also hauled wood for charcoal.

While Parker was working his own land as well as the additional jobs, squatters were becoming a growing problem in that part of Utah and it was only a matter of time before he had to deal with them. Another family of Mormons had taken up residence on a portion of the new Parker homestead and began tilling the land and raising livestock. Because there existed little in the way of formal law enforcement in that part of Utah, and because Parker was committed to following the rules established by the Mormon church, he reported the trespass to the local bishop and asked that the squatters be required to leave. In a surprising decision, the bishop judged the squatters more deserving of the land than Parker and awarded it to them. Parker had spent years, along with a great deal of money and energy developing this portion of land only to have it taken away from him by church authorities.

Having been treated unfairly, Parker had nothing to do with the Mormon church thereafter. Young Robert Parker, after witnessing the unjust actions of the bishop, harbored contempt for the Mormon church, as well as disdain for religious hypocrites for the rest of his life. In time, Robert Leroy Parker came to detest all institutions that took advantage of those who could do little about it. These included not only the Mormon church, but also banks and railroad companies.

Robert Leroy Parker was only thirteen years old when he had his first encounter with the law. At the time he was working for a rancher named Pat Ryan not far from the town of Milford. The Parker family had debts to pay, and young Robert had decided to contribute. He was described as dependable, intelligent, and capable of doing a man's work.

One payday, Robert rode into Milford to purchase a new pair of overalls. On arriving at the mercantile, he found it closed. Having already made the long journey into town and not wanting to wait around for the owner to return, he gained entrance, selected a pair of overalls, and left a note promising to return another day with payment.

Though conducted with the best intentions, the act was deemed unacceptable to the owner of the mercantile who immediately reported it as a theft. Two days later, Robert was arrested. It was eventually determined that no crime had been committed, and he was released after two days.

The incident left several important impressions on Robert Leroy Parker. First, he was worried that the allegation of theft would be embarrassing to his family, and he regretted any shame they might have to endure. Second, he was appalled at what he considered a bullying miscarriage of justice. From that point on, he harbored a certain contempt for the law.

Because he was brought up to be honest and forthcoming, Robert Parker presumed in his youthful naiveté that everyone else was also, and that others would appreciate and understand such things in their fellow man. Young Robert's lack of worldly experience was in part responsible for this cultivation of this embryonic idealism.

Just after the mercantile incident, young Parker was arrested for stealing a saddle. It was never determined whether or not he was guilty of the charge, but while he was in jail, he was badly mistreated by the sheriff of Garfield County. Angered by his treatment, Robert Parker, according to author Charles Kelly, swore vengeance then and forevermore against lawmen.[2]

Robert left the Ryan ranch and went to work on the Marshall Ranch and Dairy around 1881 or 1882. The pay was better and Robert received free milk, cheese, and butter, which he delivered to his family. According to area gossip, the Marshall Ranch served as a sometime headquarters for a gang of horse thieves and cattle rustlers. One member of this outlaw gang was a man named Mike Cassidy. Mike Cassidy had a reputation as a skilled breaker and trainer of horses. He was also an excellent shot with a handgun, reputed to have been able to put a bullet through a silver dollar at forty paces. Cassidy was also charismatic and likable, and was idolized by the area's youth who regarded him as a hero. Adults respected him and he claimed a number of good friends.

Robert Parker was fascinated with Mike Cassidy from the first time he met him at the Marshall Ranch. He was impressed with his skills related to horses and cattle. He was also taken with Cassidy's disdain for the wealthy cattle barons. In time, Robert learned of Cassidy's outlaw activities. To him, it all sounded glamorous; a life filled with excitement and a certain level of danger as opposed to the tedium and hard work associated with his menial duties on the ranch.

Outlaw Mike Cassidy also grew fond of Parker and was impressed with the youth's hard work and his skill with livestock. Cassidy spent a great deal of time with Robert, passing along his techniques for breaking and training horses. He gave Robert a saddle and instructed him in the finer points of horsemanship. In a short time, Robert was almost as skilled a rider as Cassidy.

Cassidy also presented Robert with a revolver, along with money to purchase ammunition. When they had time away from their ranch chores, Cassidy taught Robert how to handle the weapon. After weeks of practice, Robert was regarded as one of the best shots in the valley. Not long after taking Robert under his wing, Cassidy ran afoul of the law and fled to Mexico where, according to most reports, he remained until his death.

By the time Robert Leroy Parker was eighteen, he was five feet nine inches tall and weighed 155 pounds. Though strong and durable, he remained soft-spoken and friendly to all. The year was 1884, and Robert informed his family that he was leaving the area, that he wanted to seek opportunities above and beyond what was available to him in Utah. He said he was going to Telluride, Colorado, to seek work in the mines.

On arriving in Telluride, Robert, who was now calling himself Roy, secured a job loading ore onto pack mules and transporting it from the mines to the mills. When he received his paycheck, he always sent a portion of it home to his family.

Shortly after coming to Telluride, Parker sold his mare and made an arrangement with a local rancher to board an unbroken colt he had acquired. Several months later when he could get some time off from his job, Parker took it upon himself to break the colt. He made several visits to the ranch, and each time the rancher offered to purchase the animal, but was always turned down. One evening when Parker went to the pasture, he took the colt to a different location to work with him. The rancher charged Parker with horse theft and requested he be arrested. The rancher stated that the colt belonged to him and that he could produce several witnesses to testify that it was so.

Parker had no choice but to leave the area. He was arrested a short time later and placed in the county jail at Montrose. During a subsequent trial, Parker was found innocent of the charge. Shortly thereafter, he left Colorado for Wyoming. After working many odd jobs, he traveled to Miles City, Montana. With few promising prospects, he decided to return to Colorado and made his way back to Telluride. While working at a number of tedious ill-paying jobs, he met Matt Warner, another refugee from Utah and a recovered Mormon. The two became fast friends.

Warner earned his living racing horses. As Parker was a splendid horseman, the two teamed up. During a racing event in Cortez, Colorado, Parker made the acquaintance of Tom McCarty, Warner's brother-in-law. McCarty had a reputation as a horse thief, rustler, and gambler, and some are convinced he also robbed at least one bank. Some writers have also posited that McCarty and Warner were once members of Mike Cassidy's gang.

Most historical accounts have Robert Leroy Parker, aka Roy Parker, and Matt Warner robbing the San Miguel Valley Bank in Telluride. Some writers claim the two were accompanied by Harry Longabaugh, known as the Sundance Kid, and Bert Madden, a sometime member of the notorious Wild Bunch. Additional research suggests that Dan Parker, brother to Robert, and a man named Bert Charter may have also been involved in the robbery. The robbers got away with $31,000. In no time at all, wanted posters were out for the participants in the bank robbery. Robert Leroy Parker was now officially an outlaw.

Some researchers are convinced that this same gang robbed a train soon after, but evidence for such is scant. Parker, along with Warner and McCarty, traveled to Brown's Park (also known as Brown's Hole) located near a point where the borders of Colorado, Utah, and Wyoming come together. By the time the three had arrived at Brown's Park, Parker had decided to change his name. He now called himself Roy Cassidy, taking the surname of the man who had been such a big influence on him. A few weeks later, he changed his name again, this time to George Cassidy.

Eventually, George Cassidy found work on the Bassett Ranch in Wyoming, where he met and became friends with Elzy Lay. Cassidy and Lay had much in common—both were skilled horsemen and hard workers. In search of a better job with better pay, Cassidy made his way to Rock Springs, Wyoming, where he found work at Gottshe's Butcher Shop. In a very short time, the customers were calling him Butcher Cassidy, which was soon shortened to "Butch." The nickname stuck, and from that point on Robert Leroy Parker was Butch Cassidy.

In time, Butch Cassidy found himself hanging out with men who were to become known as the Wild Bunch and the Hole-in-the-Wall Gang. They included Harry Longabaugh, Elzy Lay, Matt Warner, and others. All were men who had run afoul of the establishment one way or another. They planned bank and train robberies, not only for the money but also to thumb their noses at corporations such as the railroad companies, the banks, and law enforcement, institutions that Cassidy and others were convinced preyed upon the working class. In particular, Butch Cassidy was eager to rob trains, and he soon found opportunities to do so.

WILCOX, WYOMING

Wilcox, Wyoming, is located sixty miles northwest of Laramie in the southeastern part of the state. So small and insignificant is Wilcox today, it is not even noted on most state maps. In 1899, it was little more than a trackside station and water stop manned by one or two railroad employees. On June 2 of that year, however, it entered the history books as the scene of a noted train robbery, one that some historians are convinced was perpetrated by members of the Wild Bunch, including Butch Cassidy, Will Carver, Ben Kilpatrick, Elzy Lay, Harvey "Kid Curry" Logan, Logan's brother Lonnie, and George "Flat Nose" Currie. Harry Longabaugh, the "Sundance Kid," may also have been involved, but this has never been verified. While the majority of researchers agree that Butch Cassidy and the Wild Bunch were responsible for the Wilcox train robbery, details of the event remain controversial, and accounts differ.

It is generally agreed that the train robbers halted the westbound Union Pacific Overland Limited No. 1 at 2:09 a.m. near Wilcox by standing on the tracks and swinging a red lantern, the accepted signal to stop, usually associated with a hazard ahead. Once the train came to a halt, two men wearing masks—believed to be Cassidy and Harvey Logan—climbed into the cab and pointed their revolvers at the engineer W. R. Jones and the fireman, a man named Dietrick. Jones was ordered to take the train across a bridge a short distance away. Standing up to the robbers, Jones refused. At that point, Logan pulled a knife and slashed the engineer across the face. Bleeding from the cut, Jones acquiesced to the demand and started the train forward. Moments later, the entire train crossed the bridge. Once on the other side, Jones was instructed to halt the train. As he did so, an explosion was heard behind the train. The outlaws had rigged the bridge with dynamite, but the explosion failed to collapse it into the ravine below. It is believed that they were convinced that another train would soon follow the Union Pacific and wanted to make certain it would not be able to catch up to them.

Members of the gang uncoupled the passenger coaches from the express and mail cars and ordered Jones to move the train another two miles up the track where he was to stop. At that point, four additional outlaws rode up brandishing revolvers and rifles. Remaining on their horses, they stood guard over the train.

Cassidy, Logan, and at least one other robber walked over to the express car and banged on the door, yelling for the messenger to open it. The messenger, Ernest Charles Woodcock, refused and made certain the door was fully bolted shut. Neither having the time nor the willingness to negotiate, the robbers placed a charge of dynamite at the bottom of the door, lit the fuse, and retreated several yards away. The resulting explosion blew the large iron door several yards from the tracks and pieces of the express car one hundred yards in all directions. One end of the adjacent mail car and a number of bridge supports behind the train were also destroyed.

Miraculously, messenger Woodcock, though injured, survived the explosion. He suffered several cuts and a possible concussion. On spotting the semiconscious messenger lying on the floor of the car, at least one of the outlaws wanted to shoot him, but Cassidy interfered stating that the courageous messenger deserved to live. Besides, he said, he possessed the combination to the safe, which was the target of the robbery.

The bleeding and dazed Woodcock was revived by the robbers and, when ordered to open the safe, refused. Wasting no time, the robbers attached a charge of dynamite to the safe and blew away the thick steel door. In the process, they destroyed much of what was left of the express car. When the safe exploded, the money inside was blown into the air where it was scattered by the wind, forcing the robbers to chase after it, plucking it out of the air and scooping it up from the ground.

After stuffing the bills into their saddlebags, the outlaws signaled their companions who were standing guard near the locomotive that it was time to leave. Moments later they were riding away to the north toward Caspar. The train robbers got away with over $3,000.

It was only one hour before sunrise on June 2, 1899, when Union Pacific Railroad authorities were notified of the heist. Officials immediately suspected the Wild Bunch was behind the train robbery.

Riding from the scene of the crime, the outlaws split up and headed off in different directions. Posses were formed as soon as word of the robbery spread, but by the time they arrived at the scene of the crime the trail had grown cold. Between the robbery and the arrival of the lawmen, a heavy rain struck the area and washed away any tracks. In time, four hundred men joined the pursuit of the robbers. It was estimated that during their escape, the Wild Bunch traveled over 1,500 miles while evading the posses. Union Pacific Railroad detective, F. M. Hans, was quoted as stating: "Time and again [the robbers] have been surrounded by ten times their number, yet by the display of their desperate nerve and knowledge of woodcraft have managed each time to get away."[3]

According to Hans, the robbers ". . . kept on into the Big Horn Basin, then turned back and retraced their steps through the Powder River country into the Jackson's Hole country, the wildest and most desolate stretch of mountainous country in the West."[4]

The Union Pacific Railroad and Pacific Express companies jointly offered rewards of $2,000 for each of the train robbers, dead or alive. The US government joined in with a $1,000 reward for each outlaw. Though more than $30,000 was blown out of the safe, railroad authorities insisted that the robbers escaped with very little of the money, and that most of it was either destroyed by the explosion or scattered by the winds. None of the outlaws were captured.

WAGNER, MONTANA

While history has long recorded this next train robbery as having taken place in Wagner, Montana, in truth it occurred at a location called Exeter Switch, two miles east of the town. The robbery is notable for at least two reasons. First, one of the participants was Butch Cassidy. Second, it was the last train robbery perpetrated in Montana by the gang known as the Wild Bunch.

Wagner is located in northeastern Montana nine miles west of Malta and originally set alongside the Northern Pacific Railroad line. Today, Wagner is a small, unincorporated village on State Highway 2 with few residents.

Around midday on July 3, 1901, the eastbound Great Northern Coast Flyer was stopped and robbed by members of the Wild Bunch. It has never been entirely clear which members were involved, but the available evidence suggests it included Butch Cassidy, Bill Carver, and either Ben Kilpatrick, Harvey "Kid Curry" Logan, or O. C. Hanks. According to witnesses, there were at least three men involved, though some accounts provide for the possibility of more. Some writers insist Harry Longabaugh—the Sundance Kid—participated in this robbery, but there is no evidence to indicate he was involved.

It was presumed the mastermind behind the Wagner train robbery was Harvey "Kid Curry" Logan. Logan was familiar with the area, having worked on nearby ranches, and it is believed he had had previous train robbery experience. Others have suggested the idea to rob the Great Northern train came from Cassidy, who was fond of targeting major corporations.

Though much has been written about this train robbery and its participants, the actual truth of what happened is hard to come by. For instance, confusion exists relative to how the train was actually halted. One account states it was flagged to a stop near Exeter Switch and subsequently robbed. Another account maintains that one of the outlaws (most believe it was Ben Kilpatrick) either snuck aboard one of the coaches or jumped onto a blind, made his way across the tender, jumped down into the locomotive cab, and held the engineer at gunpoint. The argument has also been advanced that both of the above occurred. (Another account has Harvey Logan purchasing a train ticket and riding in one of the coaches before exiting and making his way toward the locomotive.)

Once the train was stopped, the outlaws walked toward the express car, all the while firing their handguns at the passenger coaches to keep the occupants ducking for cover. Several were wounded by stray bullets and ricochets. Once the express car was identified, the outlaws had it uncoupled from the rest of the train and ordered the engineer to pull forward two hundred yards.

Breaking into the express car was accomplished with little difficulty, but once inside, the robbers encountered a locked safe and a messenger who was unable to provide access. Oddly, they were encountering Ernest Charles Woodcock, the same messenger who had been in charge of the express car during the Wilcox train robbery two years earlier. A small charge of dynamite was applied but it had no effect. Another was tried, and finally after four attempts the safe was finally opened and the contents withdrawn and placed in canvas bags carried by the robbers. Estimates of the amount taken in the robbery have ranged from $40,000 to $83,000 in bank notes, a consignment to the Montana National Bank in Helena. Most researchers believe the smaller amount is the correct one.

As the robbery was taking place, one of the passengers climbed out of the car and began shouting at the outlaws, and at one point fired a revolver at them. It was later determined he was a Montana sheriff. The robbers responded by returning fire with a volley and forcing the lawman back into the coach. On another occasion, one of the outlaws spotted someone leaning out of a passenger car window. Perceiving a threat, the outlaw raised his rifle and fired at the person. Unfortunately, he wounded an eighteen-year-old girl.

The bags of loot were carried to nearby horses and tied onto the backs of the saddles. The outlaws mounted up and rode across the nearby Milk River and continued south before turning east into what is today the Charles M. Russell National Wildlife Refuge. Lawmen who took up the chase conceded that the train robbers were "far better mounted than their pursuers, have already crossed the Missouri River, and are well on their way toward the 'Hole in the Wall' country in Wyoming."[5]

Other lawmen argued that the robbers made their way to the "Bad Lands along the Missouri River, near the Little Rockies, and are there awaiting the time when the chase will have grown cold."[6] In time, the robbers, at least some of them, made their way to Miles City where they spent some of the bank notes on fresh horses.

Not long after the robbery, the gang split up. A posse led by Sheriff Elijah Briant caught up with and killed Bill Carver. On December 12, 1901, Ben Kilpatrick was located and arrested in Knoxville, Tennessee. Kilpatrick was eventually tried and sent to prison. On December 13, Harvey Logan found himself involved in a shootout in Knoxville wherein he killed two policemen and escaped.

Butch Cassidy went on to great outlaw fame and was eventually glorified in books and movies. Years later, reports were received that he and the Sundance Kid were killed in a shootout with Bolivian police. Subsequent investigations found this to be fiction, and the prevailing evidence is that Cassidy returned from Bolivia to live out his life in the western United States under an assumed name.

8

Black Jack Ketchum

I<small>T CAN BE ARGUED THAT THE CRIMINAL BUSINESS OF TRAIN ROBBERY</small> attracted the likes of men who were predestined for outlaw fame—fearless and daring men who possessed a sense of adventure. It can likewise be argued that the successful train robberies themselves generated the notoriety and recognition for which many well-known bad men have been associated: Frank and Jesse James, Butch Cassidy and the Sundance Kid, Sam Bass, Rube Burrow, and others all held reputations as daring and successful train robbers.

A lesser-known train robber, but no less colorful, was Thomas Edward "Black Jack" Ketchum, regarded by many as a significant and dangerous outlaw scourge of the American West. Ketchum, along with his brother, Sam, were well known to lawmen throughout much of Wyoming and Colorado, but during most of their criminal careers, never gained the reputation such as that accorded to James and Cassidy.

Thomas Ketchum was born near China Creek on October 31, 1863, in San Saba County in the northern part of the Texas Hill Country. (At least one report says he was born in 1866.) Ketchum's father died when he was only five years old, and his mother, who was blind, passed away when he was ten, thus causing him to be shunted from relative to relative. Tom's older brother, Green Berry Ketchum, became a successful rancher and breeder of horses in the area. Another brother, Sam, married and fathered two children. When Tom decided to depart the family fold and travel west to try to make it on his own, Sam left his family and joined him. Initially, the two men found work as ranch hands in West Texas and

Black Jack Ketchum

northern New Mexico and participated in a number of cattle drives into Colorado and Wyoming.

However, by 1892 Tom and Sam had committed themselves to a life of outlawry. Along with several other members of what was referred to as the "Black Jack Ketchum Gang," they held up and robbed an Atchison, Topeka & Santa Fe train near Deming, New Mexico. They got away with an estimated $20,000. Even though attributed to the Ketchum brothers, it is unclear what role, if any, Tom or Sam had in this holdup.

Over the next several years, Tom and Sam Ketchum, while occasionally finding work on cattle ranches, preferred pursuing their criminal activities, finding it more lucrative and offering more adventure than working. They, and/or their gang members, were responsible for several murders and train robberies.

Oddly, both Tom and Sam were referred to as "Black Jack" at various times, often generating a level of confusion among researchers relative to what brother participated in which holdup and to what degree. Though it is suspected they were both involved in several train robberies together, there is little on record to substantiate this contention. At times, both Tom and Sam rode with Butch Cassidy, Elzy Lay, Harry Longabaugh, and other members of the Wild Bunch. Records indicate the two participated in train robberies perpetrated by the Wild Bunch but likely had minor roles in those events. There is little doubt, however, that the brothers learned much about the criminal trade from Cassidy and other gang members. When not riding with the Wild Bunch, Tom, sometimes accompanied by his brother or other gang members he recruited, indulged in robbing sprees. By late 1895 former Wild Bunch member Harvey "Kid Curry" Logan had also become a member of Tom's gang of bandits.

Of the two brothers, Tom was the most recognized and, in the end, generated the most publicity and notoriety. He was regarded by most who were acquainted with him as crazy, often exhibiting behavior considered bizarre even by the standards held by the most hardened outlaws. Today Tom Ketchum would be referred to as a psychopath. The clearly deranged man was considered far too outrageous, dangerous, and unpredictable even for most of the members of the Wild Bunch, no strangers to violent men, killing, and related activity.

On more than one occasion, Ketchum was observed beating himself over the head with his own revolver and lashing himself across the neck and back with his lariat, self-inflicted punishment for some mistake he determined was his fault. Once, when a woman he had been seeing decided she wanted nothing to do with him, Ketchum, in front of gang members, beat himself bloody with the butt of his revolver.

Black Jack Ketchum was also known to drink heavily. Sometimes by himself and other times with companions, he would remain drunk for long periods of time, the alcohol making him more belligerent, bellicose, and aggressive than he normally was.

It was just a matter of time before Black Jack Ketchum returned to his home state of Texas to rob a train.

LOZIER STATION, TEXAS

On May 14, 1897, Thomas "Black Jack" Ketchum, along with two unidentified companions, robbed a Southern Pacific train near the remote and lonely Lozier Station in the Big Bend Country of West Texas and 250 straight-line miles west of San Antonio. Though unidentified, it is believed by many that one of Ketchum's partners was Ben Kilpatrick. Kilpatrick had previous train robbery experience as a part-time member of the Wild Bunch. Years later, Kilpatrick, after serving a prison sentence, would return to that part of West Texas to attempt another robbery of this same train. It would prove to be his last successful heist.

At 2 a.m. on the morning of May 14, the Southern Pacific Sunset Limited made an emergency stop at the unmanned Lozier siding. Less than an hour earlier, the train had pulled out of Del Rio near the Mexican border and was westbound for El Paso. Several minutes after leaving Del Rio, the engineer, a man named Freese, told the conductor, named Burns, that the train was running erratically. Since the next station down the line was Lozier, Freese recommended they stop there and try to determine the problem. After pulling into the station, Freese and the conductor examined the train to locate the disturbance. As the men were thus occupied, the fireman, a man named Bochat, topped off the water tank from the supply positioned next to the tracks.

Several dozen yards behind the engine and coal tender and at least one passenger car was the express car. Wells Fargo messenger Henry Boyce was in the final stages of conducting an inventory of the shipment that had been placed on board at Del Rio. The shipment consisted of more than $90,000 in paper currency and a bit more than $6,000 in silver coins. Boyce carefully placed the shipment into the safe, which was then closed and locked.

As the engineer and conductor went about their inspection, their movements were observed by a trio of men from within the deep shadows of the station building a short distance away. One of the men was Thomas "Black Jack" Ketchum. By this time, Ketchum was an acknowledged criminal who made his reputation as a train robber in Colorado and Wyoming. Because of continual scrapes with the law in those states, as well as the fact that he was heavily pursued, Ketchum had drifted south with his gang into Texas, where he was less known.

It took Freese and Burns an hour to detect the problem with the engine and correct it. Shortly after climbing back into the locomotive, the engineer gave the signal to proceed and the train was under way. As it began the slow departure from the station, the outlaws struck. Ketchum, carrying a knapsack and a rifle, and accompanied by one of his partners, dashed from his hiding place and leaped onto one of the railroad cars. The two men climbed the ladder to the roof and made their way over several more cars toward the engine.

As Ketchum and his companion were creeping forward, the outlaw remaining behind cut the telegraph wire that connected this station to others down the line. This done, he dashed several dozen yards away and down into a shallow draw where the bandits' horses had been hobbled. After removing the fetters, the outlaw mounted his own and led the other two out of the draw and along the tracks behind the train.

By the time the train had traveled five miles, Ketchum and his companion had reached the coal tender, crossed it, and jumped down into the cab of the locomotive. Ketchum pointed his rifle at engineer Freese and ordered him to stop the train. Conductor Burns, who was accompanying

Freese in the cab, along with the fireman, Bochat, were held at gunpoint by the second outlaw. When the train came to a stop, Ketchum forced Freese, Burns, and Bochat out of the cab and instructed them to stand next to the tracks. Ketchum descended the cab and ordered Freese to lead him to the express car. Freese led the way. Ketchum followed, the tip of his rifle barrel just inches from Freese's head.

On reaching the express car, which was pointed out to him by Freese, Ketchum banged on the door with the butt of his rifle and demanded messenger Boyce open it. The outlaw received no response. Twice more Ketchum called out only to be greeted with silence. Growing annoyed and angry, Ketchum crawled beneath the express car, cocked his rifle, and fired a round up through the wooden floor. Believing he had finally secured Boyce's attention, he yelled for the messenger to open the door or he would shoot Freese through the head.

Again, Ketchum received no response from Boyce. Concerned about the potential fate of the engineer, fireman Bochat, who had been watching from his position near the locomotive, tentatively approached the express car and begged Boyce to open the door. He explained that Ketchum was quite serious about his threat to kill the engineer if he did not. Following several tense seconds, Ketchum and the railroad employees could hear the inside latches being released. A moment later, the express car door slid open, and Boyce stepped up to the opening with his hands raised. Ketchum pulled his revolver from its holster, pointed it at Boyce, and ordered him to step to the rear of the car. This done, Ketchum climbed into the car.

Once inside the express car, Ketchum ordered Boyce to open the safe. When Boyce said that he did not know the combination, Ketchum placed the barrel of his rifle against the messenger's neck. Nervous and shaking, Boyce explained that the only person who knew the combination was the relief messenger in El Paso, and that such a procedure was now railroad company policy.

Angered even more at this revelation, Ketchum knocked Boyce to the floor. From his own coat pocket, the outlaw withdrew four sticks of dynamite, all tied together in a bundle. Setting down his rifle, he knelt in front of the safe, attached the explosives to the heavy metal door, and lit the fuse. Rising, he approached Boyce, tossed him from the express car, and leaped to the ground after him. As the dynamite fuse burned, Ketchum ran for the shelter of some nearby rocks. As he did, he warned Freese, Burns, Bochat, and Boyce to take cover.

A few seconds later, the surrounding desert vibrated from the sound of the huge explosion and smoke billowed out of the opening of the express car. When it cleared, Ketchum reentered the car. He found the door to the safe completely blown away but the contents within remarkably undisturbed.

Ketchum filled his knapsack and saddlebags with the silver coins. He checked his pocket watch and noted that ninety minutes had passed since the train had pulled away from the Lozier station. A few minutes later, the third outlaw arrived with the horses. After tying the coin-filled knapsack behind his saddle, the always unpredictable Ketchum bade a polite goodbye to Freese, Burns, Bochat, and Boyce and, along with his two companions, rode away toward the southwest in the direction of the Chisos Mountains.

As Ketchum and his gang disappeared into the desert darkness, Freese raced back to the engine, and in a short time had the train barreling toward the next stop—Sanderson. On pulling into the station, conductor Burns leaped out of the cab and informed the agent of what happened at Lozier. He instructed him to telegraph news of the robbery to Southern Pacific Railroad authorities in El Paso immediately.

By the time the sun came up, Texas Ranger Captain John R. Hughes had received information of the robbery. From the ranger encampment at Ysleta, Texas, some twenty miles downriver from El Paso, Hughes hand-picked a platoon of fifteen rangers, armed them, and supplied them with provisions to last at least a week. After assembling a string of strong and trail-hardened mounts, the rangers set out toward the robbery site.

When the Texas Ranger contingent rode up to the scene of the robbery, they found enough sign to indicate that the robbers had fled toward the southwest. After following the tracks for a short distance, however, the rangers lost them. For several days, Hughes and company searched the rugged arid country just south of the robbery site but to no avail—they were unable to find the trail of the bandits. On the fourth day, as they were circling a potential area, one of the rangers came across the tracks of three horses heading southwestward. The rangers followed the trail but lost it again, this time when it crossed a stretch of granite outcrop. For another full week, the rangers crisscrossed the area in hope of relocating the tracks of the outlaws but were unsuccessful. Captain Hughes finally called a halt to the search and returned with his charges to Ysleta.

After fleeing from the robbery site, Ketchum and his companions rode hard for two days and nights, stopping only to water and rest the horses. On the morning of the third day of flight, the gang had made its way deep into the remote and barely accessible reaches of the Big Bend country, not far from the Mexican border. Two more days of riding through deep canyons and across rugged ridges brought them to their planned destination—the isolated ranch of the Reagan brothers in Reagan Canyon.

The relationship between the four Reagan brothers and the outlaw Black Jack Ketchum was long-standing. The ranchers agreed to allow Ketchum and his gang to hide out in the area for a few days. As the train robbers unsaddled their horses, one of the ranch hands obliterated their tracks into the ranch by driving a herd of cattle over them.

Ketchum was concerned that the Texas Rangers would be searching for them and might be closing in on their hideout. It was just a matter of time, he reasoned, before they arrived. Not wanting to be caught with the $6,000 in silver coins and fearing that if he transported them in his saddlebags they would slow him down, Ketchum decided to cache the loot at some location on the ranch. After giving the Reagan brothers $200, Ketchum stuffed the remaining coins into his knapsack and carried them to a cave he had located earlier a short distance north of Reagan Canyon. The next day, the three outlaws rode away, intending to return at some future date and retrieve the treasure. None of them could have realized that they would never again see that part of Texas.

Ketchum decided it was in his best interest to put as much distance as possible between himself and the Texas Rangers, so he and his companions traveled to Colorado. Once settled into the Rocky Mountain state, the outlaws lost no time in returning to robbing trains.

On September 3, 1897, Ketchum and his gang robbed a Colorado & Southern train, making off with $3,500. On July 11, 1899, the gang struck again, robbing the same train and taking $70,000 in gold coins. It was to be the last successful robbery undertaken by Ketchum.

Following the July 11 robbery, Huerfano County (Colorado) Sheriff Farr assembled a posse consisting of nine men experienced in tracking and fighting. They were accompanied by two railroad detectives. A few days later the posse caught up with the robbers and a gunfight ensued. Two members of the gang were killed and Black Jack's brother, Sam, was wounded. Black Jack, along with Bill Franks and another man named McGinnis, escaped.

Sam Ketchum was arrested. While waiting for trial in a Santa Fe, New Mexico, jail, he contracted blood poisoning, presumably from his wound, and died. Franks was killed in San Angelo, Texas, in 1901. McGinnis was later captured, tried, and sentenced to the New Mexico penitentiary. He was pardoned in 1906. Black Jack remained at large.

Though his gang had been decimated and he suffered significant failure, Thomas "Black Jack" Ketchum was more determined than ever to return to robbing trains. His next attempt turned out to be his last.

FOLSOM, NEW MEXICO

By April 16, 1899, Black Jack Ketchum had been hiding out in New Mexico for several weeks, a location to which he escaped knowing he was being pursued by lawmen. A wanted man in Texas for train robbery, he felt relatively safe in his new location. It was in his best interest to maintain a low profile for a time, but the unpredictable and impulsive Ketchum could not resist the opportunity to rob another train. This urge, one that lacked adequate preparation, led to what would be his final robbery and, ultimately, his demise.

Ketchum was somewhat familiar with the schedules of the Colorado & Southern Railroad line in northeastern New Mexico. It is believed that he, in the company of others, had robbed C&S trains in the past. At this point, however, Ketchum, was without a gang. Rather than take the time and effort to assemble one, he decided to undertake the challenge by himself. Researchers are convinced that by this time, the deranged

Ketchum had long since entered into the realm of madness and instability. The historical record shows that train robbery attempts executed by a single bandit were rarely successful.

Ketchum rode to a location not far from the C&S station at Folsom, a lonely spot along the route from Raton to Clayton. After looking over the station and the tiny settlement nearby, he rode some distance away into a shallow canyon where he spent the night in a cave. Early the next morning he saddled his horse, mounted up, and rode back toward Folsom. At this early hour everything was quiet save for the chuffing of the eastbound C&S locomotive at the station platform as it was preparing to depart. Other than one man loading a small amount of freight into one of the cars, few people were about, and Ketchum went unnoticed as he approached. After reaching a point behind the station, he dismounted, turned his horse loose, and observed the goings-on near the train.

Moments before the C&S pulled away from the station, Ketchum dashed from behind the building, across the tracks, and boarded the baggage car from the blind side. As the train pulled away, Ketchum climbed to the top of the car and made his way forward. He reached a point atop the coal tender where he waited until the train was approximately three miles from the station. When he was convinced sufficient distance had been covered, Ketchum crawled to the front of the tender and dropped into the locomotive cab. Pointing his revolver in the face of the surprised and frightened engineer, the outlaw ordered the train stopped.

When the train halted, Ketchum forced the engineer out of the cab and marched him back to the express and mail cars. Ketchum's plan was to have the engineer uncouple the cars from the rest of the train and pull forward another mile up the track. There, the train would be stopped once again and Ketchum, at his leisure, would break into the express and baggage cars and rob them without any interference from the passengers in the trailing coaches. For reasons unknown, Ketchum was uncomfortable with this location, and before uncoupling the cars, had the engineer pull forward another mile before stopping at another location.

Ketchum erred in his choice of where to stop, however. The train was on a tight curve and in a somewhat cramped position, making it impossible for the cars to be uncoupled. Disappointed but undeterred, Ketchum climbed out of the cab and walked down to the cars he targeted. Selecting the express car, he broke in, having encountered no resistance whatsoever from the messenger. One account of the robbery has the always-volatile Ketchum shooting the express messenger in the jaw. Another account states this did not happen.

With the train stopping, starting up again, and then stopping once more, the conductor, Frank Harrington, grew convinced that a robbery was in progress. Harrington, a veteran of at least three previous robberies, had lost his patience with outlaws and was determined never to allow it to happen again. Peering out of one of the coach windows, Harrington discerned that only one robber was involved in the attempt. The conductor retrieved his shotgun, climbed out of the coach, and went after the bandit.

Ketchum had gone through the express car and found nothing worth taking. He moved on to the baggage car. When Harrington arrived at the baggage car, he could hear the robber rummaging around inside. The conductor stepped to the door, aimed his shotgun at the robber, and commanded him to desist. Reacting to this unexpected threat, Ketchum yanked his revolver from its holster and got off a hurried shot at the intruder. The bullet whizzed by Harrington's head, missing him by an inch. (Another account has Harrington being wounded by the shot.) Harrington responded to the assault by firing back at the robber.

The load of buckshot struck Ketchum in the right elbow, nearly severing the lower arm from the upper. Ketchum staggered and fell out of the baggage car onto the ground. Harrington yelled for the engineer to get the train moving as fast as possible. As the engineer manned the throttle, Harrington climbed aboard the open baggage car and, as the train sped away, watched the wounded train robber, clearly in pain, make his way to the shelter of some trees a short distance from the tracks.

The brave and daring conductor Harrington saved the train from being robbed. Little did he know at the time that the man he shot was the notorious train robber, Black Jack Ketchum. Harrington would learn several days later that he was responsible for putting an end to Ketchum's criminal career.

After attempting to rob the eastbound Colorado & Southern train near Folsom, New Mexico, on April 16, 1899, all Black Jack Ketchum had to show for his effort was a severe wound to his right arm, the lower part dangling from the upper by tendons and sinew. Dizzy and in great pain, Ketchum collapsed to the ground near the railroad tracks and waited for the inevitable posse to arrive.

The engineer for the C&S train stopped at every station along his route and had telegraphs describing the robbery attempt sent to law enforcement authorities at a number of locations. The messages advised them to be on the lookout for a badly wounded man near the location of the scene of the botched holdup. By the time the train pulled into the station at Clayton, New Mexico, the sheriff there was in the process of forming a posse. Within minutes, it was racing back toward the scene of the robbery fifty miles away. On arriving, however, the posse could not find the wounded man.

Earlier Ketchum, fearing he was dying from his wound, flagged down another train. When the train came to a stop, the brakeman spotted the lone individual, clearly in distress, near the tracks. He climbed down and approached the injured stranger, prepared to provide aid. To his shock, the man pulled his revolver and pointed it at his chest. A conductor arrived at the scene, took it all in, and said to the stranger, "We just came to help you, but if this is the way you feel, we will go and leave you."

Barely able to stand, Ketchum lowered his weapon. He told the brakeman that he was "all done," and to "take me in." Assisted by the brakeman and the conductor, Ketchum was lifted into the caboose and placed on a cot. The conductor summoned a guard to remain in the caboose with Ketchum as the train proceeded toward Folsom. On arriving, Ketchum was placed under arrest by Union County Sheriff Saturnino Pinard, who had been informed of the earlier robbery attempt.

On being entered into the arrest log, Ketchum gave his name as Frank Stevens. (One writer claims the name he provided was George Stevens.) With the limited resources available at Folsom, Ketchum's wound was cleaned and bandaged. Forty-two shotgun pellets were plucked out of his arm. As soon as it was possible to do so, the train robber was transported to San Raphael Hospital in Trinidad, Colorado, forty-five miles to the northwest. There, what remained of his forearm was amputated.

During the subsequent investigation, lawmen learned that Frank Stevens was, in truth, the notorious train robber Thomas "Black Jack" Ketchum, a man wanted in New Mexico since 1892. It was also learned that Ketchum was wanted in four other states for train robbery, bank robbery, murder, and more. When Ketchum was deemed by his doctor to be well enough to travel, he was moved to Santa Fe where he was kept in a cell until such time as he was to go to trial. During the time he was incarcerated at Santa Fe, Ketchum confessed his roles in a number of previous holdups in Texas to investigators, even to the point of providing details of the planning and execution of his crimes.

After a few weeks, Ketchum was transferred back to Clayton where he was formally charged with the attempted robbery of the C&S train near Folsom. He was tried, found guilty, and sentenced to be hanged. While in jail, Ketchum was given the opportunity to meet with a priest, but the unrepentant outlaw said, "I'm gonna die as I've lived, and you ain't gonna change me in a few minutes." To this he added, "Have someone play a fiddle when I swing off." The priest was sent away.[1]

The date for the execution was set for April 26, 1901, at 8 a.m. Black Jack Ketchum was dressed in a suit. He was heavily manacled—a heavy steel belt encircled his waist, and his good arm was cuffed to the belt. His legs were linked together with a short length of chain such that he could only shuffle forward. He was escorted by several deputies, all carrying rifles. These impressive precautions seemed rather unnecessary for a one-armed man who was barely able to move, but the sheriff was reacting to rumors that members of the Black Jack Ketchum Gang would arrive and attempt to free the captive.

Within a few seconds after Ketchum had ascended the steps of the gallows, a black hood was fitted over his head and pinned to his shirt. As the hangman on the platform secured the noose around his neck, Ketchum, in a taunting manner, said, "Hurry up, boys. Get this over with. I'll be in hell before you start breakfast, boys!" Following some final adjustments to the noose, Ketchum yelled, "Let 'er rip!"[2]

Clayton Sheriff Garcia stood by with a hatchet to sever the rope that released the trapdoor through which Ketchum would drop. It required two blows from the hatchet. As the trap door swung open, Ketchum dropped through the opening, his body plummeting toward the ground. When the limit of the rope was reached, the outlaw's head was torn from his body. His body dropped to the ground and his head, after swinging for a moment on the rope, fell and landed atop the torso and then bounced to the ground. Onlookers screamed and photographers rushed forward to record the grisly scene. Black Jack Ketchum's train robbery days were officially over. Later that day, Ketchum's remains were interred in the Clayton cemetery.

9

The Dalton Gang

OF THE TEN DALTON BROTHERS, FOUR OF THEM TURNED TO LAWLESS-
ness and generated the fearsome reputation of the gang that terrorized
railroads from Oklahoma to California and back. Grat, Emmett, Bob,
and Bill Dalton were the mainstays of the gang, and from time to time
they were joined by others, notably George "Bitter Creek" Newcomb and
Charles Bryant.

The Daltons were from Cass County, Missouri, and were relatives
of the Youngers, partners in the train and bank robbing James-Younger
Gang. There is little doubt that the Dalton brothers were influenced by
the successful criminal activities of their relatives.

The Dalton brothers did not start out as outlaws. On the contrary,
both Grat and Bob, along with brother Frank, served as US Deputy Marshals under the famous "Hanging Judge" Isaac Parker during the 1880s.
Their main job was to prevent white squatters from establishing settle-
ments and homesteads on designated Indian land in Indian Territory
(now Oklahoma). It didn't take the brothers long to realize that some of
the outlaws they were pursuing for a variety of crimes, including horse
theft and bootlegging, were making significantly more money than law
enforcement officers. In June 1890, Grat and Bob decided to enter the
business of stealing horses.

While making their rounds as marshals, the two would steal Indian
ponies, and drive them up to Kansas and sell them at a later date. The
first few attempts were successful, but on one trip Grat was arrested with
stolen ponies. The case against him was strong but he somehow managed

Grat Dalton

to have it dismissed. Part of the arrangement was that he leave Oklahoma Territory. Grat agreed to do so and headed for California. Bill decided to settle down and pursue an honest living as a rancher.

Meanwhile, brothers Bob and Emmett also found themselves wanted for horse theft. According to author Patterson, the brothers had three choices: Turn themselves in and argue for a light sentence, flee the area as Grat had done, or concentrate on becoming more successful outlaws and attempt to harvest as much money as possible.[1] Making money appealed to them more than the other choices, so the two formed a gang, which included "Bitter Creek" Newcomb, Charles Bryant, and Bill McElhanie.

The gang's first holdup was of a gambling parlor in Silver City, New Mexico. They made off with a saddlebag full of cash but were pursued by angry citizens. A brief shootout ensued and Emmett was wounded in the arm. While Emmett traveled back to Oklahoma to recover, Bob and McElhanie decided to head for California and join Grat.

Southern Pacific Railroad detective Will Smith was stationed in California, and he became aware, not only of Grat's presence and his reputation as a heavy drinker and gambler, but also of the fact that he had been joined by two additional gang members. Smith decided to keep an eye on the bunch. He expected that not much time would pass before the suspicious characters generated problems. That time was not long in coming.

ALILA, CALIFORNIA

On February 6, 1891, as the Southern Pacific Atlantic Express was pulling away from the station at Alila (now Earlimart), California, forty miles north of Bakersfield, two men jumped onto the blind of the baggage car, climbed to the roof, and made their way toward the engine. Dropping into the cab, they pointed their revolvers at the engineer and fireman and demanded the train be stopped.

After walking back to the express car, the robbers hammered on the door and ordered the messenger to open it. Wells, Fargo messenger C. C. Haswell resisted, prompting the bandits to fire through the wooden slats of the door. Haswell was struck and suffered a head wound. With blood streaming down his face, he heroically returned fire. Somehow during the melee, the fireman, a man named Radcliff, was shot in the stomach, an accidental bullet fired by the messenger.

The robbers were unable to convince Haswell to cease firing and open the door, so they fled into the nearby brush. Oddly, Haswell was subsequently charged with shooting the fireman. During his trial, the messenger claimed that there were three robbers, one of them stationed on the opposite side of the express car, and that he had accidently shot Radcliff. Haswell was acquitted.

Railroad detective Smith immediately suspected the Dalton Gang of the attempted holdup and arrested Grat. The other members of the gang, Bob Dalton and McElhanie, were never located. It was later learned they were hiding out at Bill's ranch.

One week following the holdup, a pair of spurs was found at a remote campsite believed to have been occupied by the robbers. The owner of the spurs was identified, and he informed law enforcement authorities that he had lent them to Bill Dalton and that they had been used by both Grat and Bob. The evidence was submitted to the Tulare County grand jury and an indictment issued for all four Dalton brothers, even though Emmett had not been within fifteen hundred miles of the robbery site. Bill and Grat were arrested, but Bob and McElhanie had escaped to Indian Territory.

Grat was eventually found guilty of the Alila robbery, but the cases against the other gang members proved to be too weak to pursue. Years later, Emmett Dalton claimed that neither he nor his brother were involved in the Alila robbery. While most researchers are convinced the Daltons were behind the holdup, the event is fraught with controversy to this day. Emmett insisted the first train robbery perpetrated by the Dalton Gang took place at Wharton, Indian Territory.

It may turn out that Emmett was correct. While most researchers are convinced the Dalton Gang was behind the Alila train robbery, recent research has developed evidence that it may have been committed by two little-known outlaws named Chris Evans and John Sontag.

WHARTON, INDIAN TERRITORY

Like the Alila, California, train robbery, the holdup of an express car on the Santa Fe Railroad at Wharton, Indian Territory (now Perry, Oklahoma) on May 9, 1891, remains controversial. It is believed the Dalton Gang somehow learned there would be a significant shipment of money in the express car and decided to go after it. At this time the gang consisted of Emmett, Bob, Newcomb, and Bryant.

After stopping the train, the outlaws uncoupled the express car from those trailing it, climbed into the locomotive cab, and instructed the engineer to pull forward another half-mile down the track. This done, they returned to the express car, engineer in tow, and ordered the messenger to open up. Unknown to the Daltons, while the train was being pulled the short distance ahead, the messenger suspected a robbery was about to take place and hid most of the money and other valuable shipments. The Daltons accumulated what they thought was the entire shipment, mounted up, and rode away.

Once they were two miles from the robbery site, the gang stopped to divide the loot and realized they had been deceived, likely by the messenger. Most of the bags contained worthless paper. During an interview years later, Emmett Dalton claimed they had taken $14,000 in the robbery. Sources associated with the express company estimated the loss to be between $500 and $1,750.

Convinced it was necessary to lay low following the robbery, the gang decided to hide out near Beaver Creek, about ten miles south of Wharton. One afternoon, one of the gang members spotted a herd of horses at a nearby ranch and decided to steal ten of them. Not expecting pursuit, the outlaws were surprised when a small posse consisting of the rancher and a handful of his neighbors caught up with them. A brief gunfight ensued, with one of the ranchers killed and another wounded. The gang's crimes had just gone up a level.

Later, gang member Charlie Bryant was diagnosed with an advanced case of venereal disease and had to be hospitalized in Hennessy. He was recognized and arrested. During a subsequent escape attempt, he was shot and killed. Grat wasted no time in recruiting brother Bill to take Bryant's place, and then added two more men to the gang. With seven competent outlaws, Grat turned his attention to robbing a Kansas and Texas Railroad express car at Leliatta, Indian Territory.

LELIATTA, INDIAN TERRITORY

Leliatta was a small community during the latter part of the 1880s and the early part of the 1900s and was located between Pryor and Muskogee in the eastern part of what is now Oklahoma. Today, it is small enough to be left off most maps. On the evening of September 15, 1891, Leliatta was the focus of the holdup of a southbound Kansas and Texas passenger train by the Dalton Gang.

Learning from previous robberies, the express car company had developed a policy of locking the safe carrying cash and other valuables at the point of departure, with the only other key being in the possession of the company agent at the end of the run. The express car messenger had no access to the safe whatsoever. On this run, there were two safes, one large and one small.

Days before the robbery, Bob Dalton learned that the train was carrying a significant amount of cash, the profits from a large and successful sale of cotton. As the gang made their way toward Leliatta, they encountered a husband and wife, a couple down on their luck and traveling on foot. They were preparing to make camp for the night alongside the railroad tracks. The man was searching for stray pieces of coal near the tracks to fuel a fire so they could prepare a meal. Bob Dalton paused to exchange a few words with the man, learned what he was about, and promised him that he would be able to find abundant coal a short distance ahead after the train passed.

Two hours later, the Dalton Gang stopped the train and broke into the express car. When the messenger made it clear that he was unable to open the safes, the robbers decided to break into them. The larger one proved impossible, so they shoved the smaller one out of the car and managed to open it. Inside, they found $2,500, stuffed it into their saddlebags, and made ready to depart. Before leaving, however, Bob Dalton walked over to the locomotive and instructed the fireman to toss a couple of shovels of coal next to the tracks.

At a campsite on the morning following the robbery, the gang divided the take. An argument broke out over the split, and Bob Dalton, angered by the disagreements, informed everyone he was disbanding the gang. Later, each man rode off in a different direction. One of the gang members was an enterprising young outlaw and budding train robber named Bill Doolin (see Chapter 10, The Doolin Gang).

It was only a matter of time before the original gang reassembled. Grat, who had been jailed in California, escaped and fled back to Indian Territory, where he reunited with Bob and Emmett. Talk soon turned to robbing trains, and the trio decided to hold up a Santa Fe Express near the town of Red Rock.

RED ROCK, INDIAN TERRITORY

Red Rock, Oklahoma, (also spelled Redrock) is located in Noble County between Ponca City and Stillwater. Word had reached law enforcement authorities that the Dalton Gang was planning to rob the northbound Santa Fe. In response, several armed detectives employed by both the Santa Fe line as well as Wells, Fargo were placed on the train.

On June 1, 1892, as the train pulled into the Red Rock station, one of the gang members noticed that the normally lighted passenger coach was dark. This aroused suspicion, and the gang decided to abandon their plans and ride away. They had not gotten far when they heard the whistle of another oncoming train. Peering into the darkness, they noticed that it was, in fact, an additional section of the first train. The passenger coaches were lighted as usual. The first section had been designed to lure the bandits close enough to ambush. The Daltons decided to bide their time and wait to see what transpired.

Assuming no robbery was going to take place, the detectives relaxed their guard, and before long the train began to pull away from the station. Two of the gang members raced out of hiding and jumped aboard the engine cab and, at gunpoint, ordered the engineer, Carl Mack, to continue down the track about a quarter mile to some stock pens and stop. Mack and the fireman, Frank Rogers, were forced out of the cab and marched at gunpoint down to the express car. They were soon joined by the rest of the gang.

Inside the express car, Wells, Fargo messenger E. C. Whittlesey and guard J. A. Riehl were troubled by the sudden stoppage of the train and suspected a robbery. They doused the lights and prepared for an attack on the car. A moment later, the outlaws demanded the messenger open the door. When Whittlesey refused, the gang began firing their weapons through the windows. The messenger and guard took shelter behind some packages and fired back. Gang members crawled under the express car and fired up through the floor. During the ten-minute exchange not a single person was hit.

One of the gang members located an axe and began chopping away at the express car door, eventually creating an opening two feet wide. Fireman Rogers was ordered to crawl through the opening. Engineer Mack pleaded with Whittlesy to stop firing lest he kill Rogers. Whittlesey and the guard surrendered, and the outlaws entered the car with a sledgehammer and chisel. Using the tools, they opened the two safes, gathered the contents, placed them in bags, and departed, riding off toward the southwest.

As posses scoured the countryside for a sign of the outlaws, a report was released stating that the Daltons had taken $50,000 in the robbery. A week later this amount was reduced to $5,000, and a week after that $2,000. During an interview years later, Emmitt Dalton claimed the gang got away with $11,000. Emmitt was known to exaggerate, and the express companies were loathe to report the true amount taken during a robbery. To this day, no one knows exactly how much money was taken.

ADAIR, INDIAN TERRITORY

Adair, Indian Territory, was located in Mayse County, ten miles north of Pryor. The Missouri-Kansas-Texas Railroad ran through this region, and the $40,000 reputed to be carried in the express car on July 15, 1892, presented a strong temptation to the Dalton Gang. Initially, they had planned to rob the train at Pryor, but their nearby camp was spotted by a local farmer. Concerned the farmer might alert the authorities, the gang moved north to the tiny settlement of Adair.

The gang stormed the depot, subdued any and all found within, and awaited the train, which was scheduled to stop and take on water. Later, when the train pulled to a halt, the robbers left the depot and approached it, only to be fired upon by three deputies and a railroad detective, who were hiding in a nearby shed. The gang members responded in kind.

While some of the gang exchanged fire with the lawmen, three of the outlaws crossed the tracks and ran to the opposite side of the express car. With little trouble they broke in, attached dynamite to the safe, and blew it open. According to unverified reports, they made off with $40,000 in cash. Meanwhile, the gun battle between the outlaws and the lawmen continued to rage for a time, and then slowed to a stop when all four of the men inside the thin-walled shed were wounded. Stray bullets also wounded at least two men seated at one of the nearby town's establishments, one of whom died. As far as is known, none of the gang members were hit. During the lull in the fighting, the outlaws loaded their loot onto the horses, mounted up, and rode away.

Several major railroads and express companies had grown weary of train robbers, particularly the Dalton Gang, and were determined to do something about it. They hired noted man hunter Fred Dodge, a Special Officer for Wells, Fargo & Company. Dodge was given the charge of capturing, killing, and/or driving out of business the Dalton Gang. Dodge enlisted the aid of Heck Thomas, a US Deputy Marshal, and Burrell Cox, a famous tracker. In addition, several seasoned gunmen were added to the posse. Though this formidable group rode hundreds of miles in pursuit of the Daltons, they failed to catch up to them.

Meanwhile, the Daltons decided to refrain from robbing another train for a time, preferring to provide ample time for the pursuers to tire of the chase and eventually give up. Instead, they set their sights on robbing a bank. In fact, they decided to rob two banks on the same day in Coffeeville, Kansas. Such a holdup had never been accomplished before, and it would spell the beginning of the end for the gang.

Wells, Fargo officer Fred Dodge, along with a handful of selected deputies, invested some time and energy in assessing where the Dalton Gang might strike next. They narrowed the possibilities down to three towns, Vinita and Muskogee, Oklahoma, and Coffeeville, Kansas. Dodge sent warnings to each of the towns.

In Coffeeville, a tip had been received, and law enforcement officials and city leaders developed a plan to defend the two banks—the C. M. Condon & Company Bank and the First National Bank—with volunteers, men who could be mobilized on short notice. A supply of arms and ammunitions was made available at the hardware store next to the First National Bank.

On October 5, 1892, five members of the Dalton Gang rode into Coffeeville (some researchers claim there were six riders). They wore fake mustaches but were recognized immediately. Quietly, yet effectively, word spread throughout the town that the outlaws had arrived. By the time Bob and Emmett Dalton had dismounted and walked through the front door of the First National Bank, an estimated fifteen armed townsfolk were making their way to the nearby hardware store.

Grat Dalton, along with gang members Dick Broadwell and Bill Powers walked into the Condon & Company Bank, pulled their revolvers, handed the owner, C. T. Carpenter, and a cashier, Charles M. Ball, some grain sacks and ordered them to begin stuffing them with cash. Ball claimed the time lock on the safe would not allow them into it for another several minutes. As he placed money from his drawer in one of the sacks, two of the outlaws kept a watch on the street through the large plate glass window at the front of the bank.

At the First National Bank, Bob and Emmett were walking out the front door carrying sacks of cash when they were met with a fusillade of shots fired from the nearby drug store. They turned and ran back into the bank and out the rear door. A citizen had been stationed near the back door, but before he could react to the sudden appearance of the two gang members, he was shot. The brothers raced down the alley and made their way back to where they had tied their horses. Along the way, they fired at citizens they perceived as threats, striking three.

At the Condon Bank, at least one dozen shooters were firing from the hardware store, their bullets shattering the plate glass window. Inside, the outlaws sought cover. Meanwhile, additional townsmen were taking up positions in doorways and behind obstacles, all focused on the Condon Bank.

Grat Dalton, Powers, and Broadwell exited the bank from a side door into an alley and raced out onto Walnut Street. Each man was shot over and over but somehow each was able to continue forward. After running down one-third of the block, Grat ducked under a wagon for protection. Powers attempted to take refuge in a business, but the door was locked, so he turned and ran back toward the alley on the side of the bank. Broadwell continued toward the horses but was badly wounded and staggering. He managed to climb onto his mount and ride away but was struck twice more.

From his place of concealment, Grat shot Charles Connelly, the city marshal, in the back. Bob and Emmett, running through alleys, emerged in the middle of the block. Bob was struck by a rifle bullet. He was knocked to the ground, and as he tried to stand, fired at another shooter but missed. The shooter shot again, this time striking Bob in the chest.

Grat Dalton, losing blood, crawled, and staggered toward his horse. The man who had just shot Bob took aim at Grat and fired, the bullet hitting him in the throat and breaking his neck.

Emmett, suffering only minor wounds, made his way along an alley and came out onto a street. Across from where he stood were their horses tied at a hitching rail. As he crossed, he was struck in the left hip and right arm. Somehow he climbed onto his horse and was riding out of town when a citizen fired two barrels of his shotgun into the outlaw's back. Emmett fell from his horse. By the time the smoke and dust cleared, he somehow had survived and was the only member of the gang left alive. He was tried and sentenced to prison.

The Coffeeville bank robbery attempt spelled the end of the Dalton Gang. When Emmett Dalton was released from prison years later, he granted a number of interviews and provided many of the details related to the gang's train robberies.

Bill Doolin

10

The Doolin Gang

UNLIKE THE RENO GANG, THE JAMES GANG, THE DALTON GANG, AND the Newton Gang, all of which consisted of two or more family members as well as other relatives, the Doolin Gang boasted only one member of that name—Bill Doolin. His followers came and went, and none were related to him.

William M. Doolin was born in 1858 in Johnson County in northwestern Arkansas. By all accounts he was an easygoing lad and was described as trustworthy and capable. He worked on the family homestead and found employment on neighboring farms. When Doolin was twenty-three, he migrated west and found work on ranches in Oklahoma, Kansas, and Texas. While employed as a cowhand, Doolin encountered men who would go on to become noted outlaws associated with the James and Dalton Gangs, including George "Bitter Creek" Newcomb, Charley Pierce, Bill Powers, Dick Broadwell, "Tulsa Jack" Blake, and Emmett Dalton. It was via these acquaintances that Doolin learned of experiences related to train robbery and other outlawry. The idea of robbing a train appealed to Doolin's sense of adventure.

In 1891, Doolin became a member of the Dalton Gang and participated in his first train robbery at Leliatta, Indian Territory (see Chapter 9, The Dalton Gang). Doolin proved himself to be a competent and reliable member of the gang and earned the respect of his fellow outlaws. In time, he decided to separate himself from the Daltons because he was convinced the robbery loot was not being divided fairly. He regarded himself capable of pulling off his own train robberies and consequently set about assembling a gang and selecting likely targets. He decided to rob a Missouri Pacific Express near Caney, Kansas.

CANEY, KANSAS

On October 13, 1892, a handful of well-armed outlaws led by Bill Doolin jumped aboard a Missouri Pacific train at Caney, Kansas. The gang consisted of "Bitter Creek" Newcomb, Charlie, Pierce, and Bill Raidler. After making their way across the tender, they arrived at the locomotive cab. Pointing rifles at the engineer and fireman, they demanded the train be stopped another mile down the track. This done, they ordered the engineer, a man named Eggleston, to uncouple the express car from the rest of the train and advance down the track another half-mile.

J. M. Maxwell, the express car messenger, was disturbed by the stop-and-go movement of the train so early after leaving the station. Suspecting a robbery was about to take place, he extinguished the light and prepared for the arrival of the bandits. Moments later he heard a command to open the door to the car. Maxwell remained silent, hoping the outlaws would give up and depart. Instead, they attacked the wooden car with gunfire. Maxwell was struck; his right arm shattered by a bullet. Grudgingly, he opened the door. Doolin and the others entered the car, broke into the safe, and emptied it of its contents, estimated to be around $100. Discouraged, the robbers rode away.

Despite the paltry amount of loot, the Caney, Kansas, train robbery established Bill Doolin as the leader of a gang to be feared. Over the next few years, Doolin and his followers would successfully rob more trains, as well as banks.

PONCA STATION, INDIAN TERRITORY

Bill Doolin, "Bitter Creek" Newcomb, and another noted Oklahoma outlaw named Henry Starr plotted to rob the southbound Santa Fe No. 97 passenger train at Ponca Station, a regular mail drop and water supply along the route. (Today, the town is known simply as Ponca.) Had the robbery succeeded, it would have yielded a handsome amount of cash, but it was doomed to disaster.

Somehow, word of the gang's plan leaked, and two experienced law-men placed themselves in one of the coaches. They were Wells, Fargo superintendent C. W. Stockton and Deputy US Marshal Heck Thomas. At the time, Thomas was employed as a special agent for the express company.

Unknown to and independent of Stockton and Thomas, train engineer Jack Regan and brakeman Patrick McGreeney had formulated a strategy in the event they encountered trouble along the way. If it appeared there might be the potential for a robbery, Regan would stop the train short of the station upon arrival, blow the whistle three times, and back up. McGreeny, who carried a revolver, would then join Regan in the cab.

On May 19, 1893, the three outlaws broke through the door of the station and held the four employees, along with three hangers-on, at gunpoint. One of the robbers fired a shot through the window of the telegraph office to secure the attention of the captives. Doolin informed the frightened group that they were going to rob the Santa Fe express car, and if they encountered any resistance, the hostages would be used as shields.

As the Santa Fe No. 97 approached the station, engineer Regan saw someone on the dock waving a red lantern, the sign for the train to stop. Regan grew suspicious, since Ponca was a regular stop and there was no need for such a warning. Regan let off the steam and applied the brakes, bringing the train to a stop three hundred yards short of the station. He blew the whistle three times. McGreeney, who was in one of the passenger coaches jumped from the car where he, along with a conductor, joined Regan. The three men started down the track toward the station but saw no further movement. The red lantern had disappeared.

When McGreeney reached the building, he noted it was empty. He continued toward the water tank. He had taken no more than a few steps when he was ordered to halt and raise his hands. Out of the darkness appeared three men pointing weapons at him. McGreeney recognized them as Bill Doolin, "Bitter Creek" Newcomb, and Henry Starr. (Starr was a Cherokee Indian who would later marry Myra Maybelle Shirley, better known as the outlaw Belle Starr.)

On questioning, McGreeney admitted that Stockton and Thomas had been alerted to a potential robbery and were on the train. McGreeney also informed the outlaws that Santa Fe No. 37 was on its way to the station and that it might crash into the stalled No. 97, possibly killing passengers.

The outlaws decided to walk back to the train, taking McGreeney with them. As they approached it, a voice called out behind them to halt. Turning, the outlaws saw seven US Army soldiers. They were stationed at the nearby Ponca Indian Agency and had raced to the station when they heard the earlier shot into the telegraph office. The outlaws bolted and ran toward their horses tied nearby. After mounting up, they fired several shots in the direction of the soldiers, then rode away toward the Osage Hills. The soldiers did not follow.

CIMARRON, KANSAS

The robbery of the Santa Fe California Express No. 3 by Bill Doolin and his gang yielded somewhat better results than did the Caney holdup. On June 9, 1893, the outlaws waved a red lantern at the oncoming No. 3 train as it was approaching Cimarron, Kansas, located sixteen miles west of Dodge City.

When the train halted, the engineer and fireman were ordered out of the locomotive cab and marched back to the express car. The messenger, E. C. Whittlesey, refused to adhere to the demands of the robbers to open the door. Only a year earlier, Whittlesey had been the express car messenger during the robbery committed by the Dalton Gang at Red Rock in Indian Territory. Wasting little time, the outlaws ordered the engineer to break down the door with a sledgehammer. (One account states that the robbers used dynamite to break into the car.) Though armed, Whittlesey refrained from shooting at the opening for fear of striking the engineer. Once the door was breached, the outlaws fired several rounds into the car, at least one of them injuring Whittlesey.

After entering the express car, the gang was unable to open the safe, which reputedly contained $10,000 in cash. They did, however, manage to gain access to a smaller safe, and removed an estimated $2,000. Finding no other potential for loot, the outlaws mounted up and rode away.

In a short time, a posse was formed and went in pursuit. The lawmen caught up with the robbers after crossing the Oklahoma border. During a brief exchange of gunfire, Doolin was shot in the foot, and his heel and arch were shattered. Shortly thereafter, the gang split up, and Doolin retreated to Ingalls, Kansas. There, he had a small cabin outside of town in which resided his wife, whom he had married only two months earlier. Within the few weeks following the robbery, the rest of the gang joined him there.

On August 31, 1893, lawmen eventually discovered where Doolin was hiding out. They approached his cabin and a brief gunfight ensued, but Doolin and his gang managed to escape after killing three deputies.

The Cimarron train robbery established the Doolin Gang as the successors to the Dalton Gang, the most wanted outlaws in the country at the time. Their robbery deeds dominated headlines for weeks.

DOVER, INDIAN TERRITORY

On April 3, 1895, a southbound Rock Island train slowed down to take on water at the Dover station, located sixty miles northwest of Oklahoma City. The precise identification of the outlaws who took part in the robbery is debated to this day, with most agreeing the gang consisted of "Bitter Creek" Newcomb, Charlie Pierce, Bill Raidler, "Tulsa Jack" Blake, and "Red Buck" Waightman. Though the group consisted of members of the Bill Doolin Gang, historians argue whether Doolin was present. Earlier, it had come to the attention of the gang that the train was carrying a $50,000 payroll in the safe intended for federal soldiers stationed in Texas.

As with previous robberies, the express car messenger, J. W. Jones, refused to open the door to the outlaws, who had hopped aboard the train at the previous stop. In response, the gang shot holes in the wooden side, with at least two bullets striking the messenger. In spite of the pain and bleeding, Jones continued to refuse to allow the outlaws access. When the gang members threatened to kill the entire train crew, Jones relented and threw open the door.

Once inside, the bandits ordered Jones to unlock the safe, but the messenger explained that only the express agent in Fort Worth had the key. The outlaws tried to pry open the door to the safe using tools they had brought along, but it resisted all efforts. They turned their attention to a smaller safe, as well as a pile of mailbags, but neither yielded anything of worth. Frustrated, the outlaws turned their attention to the passenger coaches, but harvested little in the way of value. As it turned out, when it became apparent that the train was being robbed, the conductor alerted the passengers and instructed them to hide their valuables under the seats. By the time they exited the coaches, the robbers had collected a total of $1,500 in cash and jewelry. Before departing, one of the robbers apologized to the passengers for robbing them, explaining that "times were hard."

The next morning a large posse set out to track the robbers. Led by famed manhunter US Deputy Marshal Chris Madsen, the group divided, one half following the tracks of the bandits while the other half took a different route hoping to intercept the outlaws near the Cimarron River. Late in the afternoon, the group following the tracks rode up on the gang napping in the shade of some trees. A gunfight lasting nearly an hour ensued, with hundreds of rounds fired. Only one man was wounded—outlaw "Tulsa Jack" Blake. After the sun went down, the outlaws rode away in the darkness.

Late in 1895, Bill Doolin, through an attorney, offered to surrender to law enforcement if he would be guaranteed a light prison sentence. The offer was rejected. Doolin decided to hide out in Eureka Springs, Arkansas. While relaxing in the warm waters of a spa, he was arrested and transported to Guthrie, Oklahoma. Newspaper reporters crowded around the jailhouse, all of them seeking stories about the now famous train robber. Doolin obliged them all with accounts of how he was misunderstood and was, he claimed, "harmless." On July 5, 1896, Doolin and several other prisoners knocked out a guard and escaped.

As with many, if not most, outlaws, things did not end well for Bill Doolin. One of the prisoners who escaped from Guthrie jail with Doolin was captured on August 4. In return for some legal favors, he informed the law enforcement authorities that Doolin was going to pick up his wife and child and take them to his mother-in-law's house in Lawton, Oklahoma, where he intended to hide out for a time before fleeing the area.

A posse of lawmen crept up to and took positions surrounding the Doolin home. In hiding, they waited for the outlaw to appear. On August 25, 1896, a wagon arrived at the home. As the driver and a helper were loading belongings into the wagon, Doolin came around the side of the house leading a horse and carrying a rifle. On spotting the outlaw, one of the lawmen called out to him to raise his hands. Instead, Doolin aimed his rifle at the sound of the voice and fired. Dropping the weapon, he pulled his handgun and fired three more shots. A second later, a volley of rifle fire cut down the train robber for good.

John Sontag

11

The Evans-Sontag Gang

During the last several decades, dozens of books have been released, both fiction and nonfiction, and many feature films, depicting the exploits and adventures of daring train robbers. The settings for the majority of these have been Wyoming and Texas, with a handful scattered across a few other western states. For reasons unclear, California has been largely ignored as a location associated with train robberies. A list of "The Greatest Train Robberies in the United States" that appeared several years ago included none from California. This seems odd, since the Golden State has served as a backdrop for several noted train robberies, along with daring and colorful robbers. Among the most prominent were Chris Evans and John Sontag. Chris Evans's origins are obscure. At various times during his life, he claimed Vermont as his birthplace. On other occasions he maintained he was born in Canada. Evans also claimed he fought in the Civil War and participated in a number of important battles while serving in the Confederate Army. He also claimed he fought with plains Indians on the Western frontier as a member of the Union Army. A diligent search for Evans's military records yielded no information on him at all, nor did he ever apply for a pension, to which he would have been entitled if he had fought in the Union Army.

Evans also told acquaintances that he once worked for the Union Pacific Railroad during the days of the westward expansion, and at other times was employed by the Central Pacific in and around Stockton, California. As with his alleged Civil War experience, documentation of these connections has never been found. Writers have maintained that Evans harbored a hatred of the Southern Pacific company as a result of his claim that the railroad overcharged him for shipping agricultural products to a market.

John Sontag, a native Minnesotan, was born John Constant. A few months following his birth, his father died and his mother married a man named Sontag, with the children assuming the name. Sontag was employed as a brakeman for the Southern Pacific Railroad. In 1887 while coupling railroad cars, Sontag sustained injuries, including a sprained back, broken ribs, and a broken ankle. Angered at his treatment by the railroad's company doctor, he became involved in a series of heated arguments. The doctors determined Sontag was fit to return to work while the patient claimed the opposite. Later, it was discovered he had embezzled money and was released by the railroad. He was tried and sentenced to prison for a short time, being let out later that same year. It was said that when he got out of prison he swore vengeance against the Southern Pacific Railroad company.

PIXLEY, CALIFORNIA

On February 22, 1889, two groups of two men, each separated by several yards, were waiting in the shadow of the Pixley, California, train station. Some were hobos and were waiting for the train to arrive so they could hop onto a blind and ride it some distance down the track. Presently, one of the men from one group approached the other group and initiated a conversation. The hobo who approached the other pair described them as "good-sized men,"[1] both wearing overcoats, and both carrying shotguns. The second pair inquired about a good place to climb onto the train and listened attentively as the first man told them. The "good-sized men" explained they were going to hunt jackrabbits. Moments later, the train arrived. The first pair climbed onto the front of the engine, while the second, now wearing masks, hoisted themselves onto the baggage section behind the tender. Later, as the train pulled away from the station, a third man came out of hiding and climbed onto one of the passenger coaches. The two men clinging to the baggage section made their way across the top of the tender and dropped into the locomotive, surprising the engineer Pete Boelenger who turned to find himself staring into the barrel of a shotgun.

Boelenger was ordered to stop the train. Once it was halted, the two hobos riding on the front of the engine suspected trouble, so they jumped off and ran into a nearby field to hide. Boelenger and the fireman were ordered out of the locomotive cab back to the Wells, Fargo express car, where the gunmen ordered the messenger, J. R. Kelly, to open the door. When Kelly refused, the robbers placed a charge of dynamite beneath the car.

As the gunmen were securing the charge, James Symington, the train's conductor, determined a robbery was taking place. He raced to the train's smoking car, where he found Modesto Deputy Sheriff Ed Bently and explained what was transpiring. Symington also recruited the brakeman, a man named Ansley, and another passenger named Gabert (also spelled Gubert), who happened to be employed by the Southern Pacific Railroad. The four men exited the coach and with two taking positions on each side of the train, made their way toward the express car.

As one of the robbers lit the fuse to the dynamite, the other spotted two men approaching, each carrying a handgun. The robber raised his shotgun and fired at the oncoming men. Gabert was struck and dropped to the ground, mortally wounded. The second pair of newcomers had reached the opposite side of the express car and was greeted by another shotgun blast, this one striking Bently. By this time, the conductor and the brakeman decided they were no match for the robbers and retreated. A moment later, the dynamite charge went off. Messenger Kelly, stunned by the explosion, continued to refuse to open the door. At this point, one of the robbers explained that if he didn't do so immediately the engineer and brakeman would be executed. Finally, Kelly slipped open the door and pushed the strongbox containing money out onto the ground. The two robbers retrieved the cash from the container and ran to their horses that were tied nearby. Details related to the amount of money taken varied, with none of the accounts in agreement other than the consensus that it was "significant." When investigators arrived at the scene, they found the body of passenger Gabert.

During the initial phases of the investigation into the robbery, it was suspected that it had been perpetrated by the Dalton Gang, which had been active in the area. Later, it was confirmed that the robbers were

Chris Evans and John Sontag, along with Sontag's brother George. It was the first of many robberies of Southern Pacific trains, each of which involved the Evans-Sontag Gang.

GOSHEN, CALIFORNIA

The Tulare County town of Goshen is located forty miles south of Fresno and was the site of the robbery of another Southern Pacific train on the evening of January 20, 1890. The robbery followed a pattern identical to that of the Pixley holdup nearly a year earlier.

The Southern Pacific passenger train No. 19 was in the process of pulling out of the station when two men, wearing masks, dashed from hiding and jumped aboard the baggage car behind the tender. (One account states that five men were involved in the robbery.) When the train had traveled two miles from Goshen, the pair jumped from the tender into the locomotive cab and instructed the engineer, S. R. DePue, to halt the train. DePue and fireman W. G. Lovejoy were then herded back to the express car, where the messenger was told to open the door and relinquish the strongbox containing the shipment of money. Perhaps aware of the injuries suffered by the messenger during the previous holdup, he followed the orders of the robbers.

After emptying the strongbox, the robbers were distracted by a movement beneath the express car. A hobo who had been hitching a ride on the undercarriage of the car dropped to the ground, scrambled away from the tracks, and began to run away. One of the robbers raised his shotgun and fired at the fleeing witness, striking him in the back, killing him. He was later identified as a Danish immigrant named Christiansen.

Newspaper accounts of the robbery reported that a total of $20,000 was taken. Little time had passed when authorities identified the robbers as the Evans-Sontag Gang. Efforts to locate and apprehend the train robbers proved futile.

CERES, CALIFORNIA

During the month of May 1891, John Sontag traveled to Minnesota to pay a visit to his brother, George. For the most part, the two men talked about robbing trains and their various experiences in doing so. Before

John undertook the return trip to California, he told George that he and Chris Evans were planning to rob a Southern Pacific train at Ceres, at the time a small community in Stanislaus County and not far from Modesto.

On September 3, 1891, two men wearing masks followed the identical pattern of the previous successful holdups in Pixley and Goshen. After jumping onto the train as it pulled away from the station, making their way across the tender, and dropping into the locomotive cab, Evans and Sontag ordered the engineer to stop the train and, forcing the fireman, a man named Charles, to accompany them at gunpoint, walked back to the Wells, Fargo express car.

After messenger U. W. Reed refused to open the door to the car, he and his assistant pulled their revolvers and took shelter, preparing to shoot it out with the robbers. Wasting little time, Evans lit a charge of dynamite and blew a hole in the side of the express car. This done, the robbers ordered the fireman to climb inside and retrieve the strong box. Messenger Reed had other ideas; he instructed Charles to leave the car or he would shoot him. Charles did so.

After the fireman left the car, Evans tossed a lighted stick of dynamite into the hole, but it failed to explode. Unknown to the robbers, Southern Pacific Railroad detective Len Harris, accompanied by an assistant, was riding in a passenger coach. When the train stopped, Harris had become suspicious and, retrieving his shotgun, left the coach and proceeded toward the express car. On spotting the attempted robbery in progress, Harris and his assistant opened fire. Evans and Sontag immediately ducked under the express car and returned fire, one of their bullets inflicting a minor injury to Harris's neck.

Realizing their apparent inability to breach the express car, Evans and Sontag ran from the train to a pair of horses tied nearby and fled toward Modesto. The pair of outlaws were disappointed with their most recent outing, but not discouraged. While they remained in hiding, they began making plans to rob more trains.

KASOTA JUNCTION, MINNESOTA

In 1892, Kasota Junction was a tiny community southwest of Minneapolis. While residing in Minnesota, George Sontag pondered the possibilities of holding up a train at the Kasota station. He contacted brother John and his partner Chris Evans to join him in the attempt. He was soon joined by Evans, but for reasons never determined, John decided not to get involved.

On July 1, 1892, Sontag and Evans stopped the train employing the usual *modus operandi*, made their way to the express car, and gained entry. At that point, the robbery attempt deteriorated; the strongbox containing the money could not be found and the express car messenger proved to be no help whatsoever. Dejected, Sontag and Evans fled the scene.

On August 1, George Sontag and Chris Evans joined John Sontag in Fresno. Once together, the trio lost little time in planning to rob the San Francisco to Los Angeles Southern Pacific passenger train No. 17 at Collis, near Fresno.

COLLIS, CALIFORNIA

Collis was a small and relatively quiet town located east of Fresno in the heart of the San Joaquin Valley. The area was given over to farming and ranching. City fathers later changed the name of the town to Kerman, and today it boasts a population of around fifteen thousand residents.

On the evening of August 3, 1892, a Southern Pacific train stopped at the station thirteen miles west of Fresno and near the town of Collis. Train robbery researchers are convinced that two men, believed to be Chris Evans and John Sontag, jumped aboard the train as it was leaving the station and, on reaching the locomotive, pointed their revolvers at the engineer, Al Phipps, and the fireman, Will Lewis. Phipps was instructed to stop the train at a designated location a short distance down the track. Not far from where the train halted stood a wagon with two horses in harness.

One of the robbers handed Phipps a small bundle of dynamite and instructed him to secure it next to "the left cylinder of the locomotive."[2] The resulting explosion damaged the engine, rendering it unable to proceed. This done, the robbers, carrying more dynamite, walked down the track to the Wells, Fargo express car. They ordered the messenger, George Roberts, to open the door to the car. When Roberts refused, the robbers set off a charge. Roberts continued to resist and a second charge was lit. This encounter continued through a total of six blasts and finally Roberts, bleeding and semiconscious, relented.

The explosions of dynamite attracted the attention of a group of farm workers who were camped near the tracks a short distance away. Curious, two of them—J. W. Kennedy and John Arnold—grabbed their rifles and went to investigate. When it was clear to the workers what was transpiring, they decided to fire their weapons at the robbers, but as it was dark, none of the bullets found targets. During the shooting, Evans and Sontag entered the express car, broke open the safe, and escaped with the contents, estimated to be between $30,000 and $50,000, an impressive amount of money at the time. They forced messenger Roberts, and Lewis, the fireman, to carry the sacks of money to the nearby wagon. This done, the robbers climbed aboard and drove away, eventually making their way to Fresno.

Despite reports describing the above events, one writer insists it would have been impossible for Evans and Sontag to breach the "triple time-locked Wells, Fargo safe."[3] Another writer insists that the money being transported in the safe consisted of Peruvian coins, though no explanation is offered as to why.

Passengers in the coaches were witnesses to the robbery, and several claimed that additional outlaws had been aiming rifles at the coaches to frighten them to remain in place. Initial reports from the railroad company that found their way into newspapers initially blamed the Dalton Gang for the robbery. When this was finally ruled out, attention shifted to Evans and Sontag, two men well known for their hatred of the Southern Pacific Railroad. Thus, the origins of what has been described as one of California's greatest manhunts was underway.

THE END OF THE EVANS-SONTAG GANG

On the day after the holdup of the Southern Pacific train at Collis, George Sontag began spending some of his loot in the Fresno and Visalia saloons. While inebriated, he bragged loud and often about his involvement in the Collis train robbery. It wasn't long before word reached law enforcement authorities. By this time, railroad detectives had connected

George and Evans with the Kasota Junction train robbery in Minnesota. On August 5, George was arrested in Visalia by Tulare County Deputy Sheriff George Witty and Southern Pacific detective Will Smith.

Once George was in custody, Witty and Smith rode a buggy out to the home of Chris Evans. As they approached the house, they spotted a man they believed to be John Sontag enter the house through the back door. When the two lawmen knocked on the front door, they were greeted by Evan's young daughter. In response to a question from Smith, she stated that Sontag was not on the premises. Smith called her a "damned little liar,"[4] pushed her aside, and entered the domicile. The daughter called out for her father.

Evans appeared and repeated that Sontag was not in the house. Witty pushed aside a nearby curtain, exposing Sontag who was pointing a shotgun at the officers. At the same time, Evans snatched up his own shotgun. The lawmen immediately turned and ran, with the outlaws in pursuit and firing their guns as they ran. Evans shot Witty in the shoulder, and when he fell to the ground the outlaw stepped up to him and placed the barrel of his revolver against his head. Witty begged for his life and Evans relented. Sontag fired at the fleeing Smith, who was struck by several shotgun pellets in the back. Evans and Sontag ran back to the house, retrieved a supply of ammunition, and escaped in the lawmen's buggy. (A second account of the encounter, based on an interview with Evan's daughter, has Witty and Smith firing first.)

When Witty and Smith returned to town, they assembled a posse that went in search of the two outlaws. They rode back to the Evans house but were unable to locate the tracks of the fleeing train robbers. The lawmen, five in all, decided to retreat a short distance from the home and wait to see if the two fugitives returned. Around midnight, Evans and Sontag, in need of supplies and food to sustain them for a period of hiding out, returned to the house. They went to the barn to pack some items and were surprised by the lawmen. A brief exchange of gunfire took place. Deputy Sheriff Oscar Beaver was killed. Evans and Sontag once again rode away.

On September 13, a second posse was organized. It consisted of six local men including Southern Pacific detective Will Smith, along with two Indian trackers called in from Arizona. Men familiar with Evans assumed he would head to the nearby mountains to hide out. The posse arrived at a location known as Young's cabin in what later became the Sequoia National Forest. They rode up to the cabin intending to stop and prepare breakfast, not realizing that Evans and Sontag were hiding inside.

As the posse members tied off their horses in the nearby brush, two of its members—Vernon "Vic" Wilson and Andrew McGinnis—walked up to the cabin intending to start a fire in the stove. Evans and Sontag, who had been watching the arrival of the lawmen, opened fire, killing Wilson and McGinnis. At the onset of the shooting, the rest of the posse took cover in the trees as Evans and Sontag ran from the cabin and into the woods in the opposite direction.

Mounting up, the remaining members of the posse pursued the outlaws but lost their trail within minutes. Following a half-hearted search, and facing an approaching cold front, the lawmen gave up and returned to town, vowing to take up the search in the spring.

On October 15, George Sontag was tried for the Collis train robbery. On October 29, a jury found him guilty after deliberating a little more than one hour. On November 3 Sontag was sentenced to a life term at Folsom Prison.

Months passed with no sign or sighting of Chris Evans and John Sontag. It is believed that many who cared little about the railroads and law enforcement were assisting the outlaws by providing food and shelter. On June 11, 1893, a four-man search party consisting of two lawmen and two citizens paused to examine an abandoned cabin in the lower foothills of Stokes Mountain in California. It had earlier been reported to the authorities that the outlaws had been using the cabin as a sometime hiding place. As the posse reined up, they spotted Evans and Sontag on foot coming out of the woods beyond and approaching the house from the back. At the same time, the fugitives spotted the lawmen and opened fire. Posseman Fred Jackson returned fire, wounding both outlaws. Evans and Sontag sought refuge behind a low pile of manure.

While Evans and Sontag cowered behind their ineffective shelter, their pursuers laid down a barrage of fire. Sontag was severely wounded in his right arm, and a second later another bullet pierced his abdomen. When Evans raised up to check on his wounded partner, he was struck in the back. The posse members could hear Sontag begging Evans to "put him out of his misery," but was refused. A second later, Evans was hit in his right arm and by a number of shotgun pellets that struck his face, tearing his right eye out of the socket.

As darkness fell, the shooting ceased as it became difficult for the posse to see the manure pile. While they listened closely for any sound from the outlaws, they heard none, though no one thought it a good idea to investigate. They would keep watch until morning.

For two hours after sunrise, the possemen watched the manure pile. Finally, after spotting no activity whatsoever, they cautiously advanced toward it, firearms at the ready. As they circled around the pile, they spotted Sontag sitting upright and partially covered by dung and straw. Apparently the outlaw had attempted to end his own life on two separate occasions, but was too weak from his wounds to manage, suffering only minor wounds. Evans was nowhere to be seen.

Sontag was taken to a hospital in Fresno. It was discovered that he had tetanus. His mother was contacted in Minnesota and days later, she arrived to care for him. John Sontag died three weeks after being admitted to the hospital.

Later, it was learned that during the dark of night Evans crawled from the hiding place all the way to Wilcox Canyon, six miles away. There he was found by a rancher named E. H. Perkins, who saw that Evans had lost a great deal of blood and was in shock. Perkins did what he could to make Evans comfortable, then rode into Visalia and informed authorities that the train robber they had been searching for was lying helpless against a haystack near his home. Evans was apprehended on the following day. He was carried to Fresno where his wounds were attended to. His recovery took weeks, and during that time his left hand had to be amputated.

On November 28, 1893, Evans stood trial for the murder of Vic Wilson during the brief gunfight at Young's cabin fourteen months earlier. Evans was sentenced to a life term at Folsom Prison. One month later, however, he, with the help of his wife and a fellow convict named Ed Morrell, who smuggled a revolver to him, escaped. On February 5, 1894, the pair was located by a posse in a forested region of Tulare County. A brief shootout took place, but the convicts escaped. They were tracked to Camp Badger where another shootout occurred, but they got away once again.

On February 19, Evans and Morrell arrived at Evans's home near Visalia. Word soon reached authorities of the arrival of the outlaws, and the following day a posse of some fifty men surrounded the house. Tulare County Sheriff Eugene Kay sent a note to Evans informing him of the size of the posse and explaining that resistance would only lead to his death. Evans and Morrell surrendered and were taken to jail. Both were returned to Folsom Prison.

On April 14, 1911, Chris Evans was paroled. He moved to Portland, Oregon, presumably with his wife, and remained there until his death at seventy years of age.

On June 27, 1893, George Sontag, along with five other Folsom inmates, attempted an escape. Using Gatling guns, prison guards fired at the fleeing prisoners, killing three, and badly wounding Sontag and another. The two surrendered. Prison officials were convinced that Sontag would die from his wounds, but after weeks he recovered, though crippled.

On March 21, 1908, George Sontag was pardoned and later found a job as a floor manager at a gambling parlor in San Francisco. Years later, he penned a book titled *A Pardoner Lifer* that was part autobiography and part sermonizing about the evils of criminal ways. In 1914 Sontag's story was made into a movie. Not long afterward, George Sontag disappeared from the public eye, and no information has been located relative to what became of him or how and when he passed.

Willis Newton

12

The Newton Gang

ACCORDING TO RAILROAD HISTORIANS, THE GREATEST TRAIN ROBBERY in the history of the United States took place in Rondout, Illinois, on June 12, 1924, where the Newton Gang heisted $3 million. It was the last major train robbery in the United States, and the last one executed by the Newton Boys.

Close to $3 million worth of currency and bonds from the Federal Reserve Bank of Chicago that was being shipped to banks in the Northeast were taken in the robbery. The heist was planned and executed primarily by Willis Newton from Uvalde, Texas, who was accompanied by his three brothers—Wylie (known as Doc), Jess, and Joe Newton, and an accomplice named Brentwood Glasscock. The Newton brothers were not only successful outlaws, they were colorful and adventurous characters who chose a life of crime over working on the farm. In addition to trains, Willis and his gang robbed more than eighty banks. They approached the business of robbing trains and banks the same as anyone committed to any other profession. And they were good at it, such that they are regarded as the most successful bank robbers in the history of the United States.

Willis Newton was born on January 19, 1889, in Cottonwood, Texas. Cottonwood was a tiny community forty-five miles southeast of Abilene in Callahan County. Willis was the sixth of eleven children of Jim and Janetta Pecos Newton.

155

Jim Newton was an itinerant farmer and sharecropper for much of his life and secured employment wherever he could find it as he traveled throughout Central and West Texas. This often meant moving from place to place. In 1903, the family of four children, along with all their belongings, packed into a wagon pulled by two horses and moved back to Cottonwood after living elsewhere, but only for a short time. Over the years, the Newtons traveled to and lived in Cisco, Fort Worth, Abilene, Big Spring, and Uvalde. In each location, Jim found work, if only for a few months.

Willis Newton, along with his siblings, knew little else but strenuous labor in the cotton fields from dawn until well past sundown. Willis was a hard worker, and as he grew into his teens he was lean, hard, and tough. His nickname was "Skinny." Though a competent field hand, Willis was convinced there were better ways to make a living. There was little to suggest at the time that Willis Newton was to grow up to earn the reputation as the most successful train robber in the history of the United States.

As a youth, Willis often left home in search of adventure and other work. He was particularly attracted to trains, and soon discovered that it was easy to climb into an empty boxcar or ride the blinds to whatever destination he had selected. Sometimes he was caught and thrown off the train, and he soon grew adept at avoiding the conductors and guards. In time, Willis grew quite familiar with trains.

During his travels, Willis often found himself in trouble with the law, some of it related to illegally riding the trains and some related to theft. Willis found it easy to break into stores and take clothes and shoes. More often than not he evaded capture, but it was just a matter of time before he was caught. In 1909 Willis was arrested for stealing a small load of cotton. He was tried, found guilty, and sent to the state penitentiary in Huntsville to serve a term of two years. After a few weeks at Huntsville, he was transferred to another prison in Rusk where he was joined by his brother, Doc, who was also serving a sentence for theft.

After serving eleven months of his sentence, Willis, along with Doc, escaped. The next day, the two fugitives broke into a store and stole some clothes, then fled on foot. Guards and trackers from the prison had been in pursuit of the brothers and caught up with them several days later, re-arrested them, and returned them to prison. Willis was sent to the penitentiary at Sugarland where he served thirty months. As a result of a series of written pleas from his mother, Willis was eventually pardoned by Texas Governor O. B. Colquitt.

A short time following his release from prison, Willis found himself in trouble once again. After returning to Uvalde, he originally obtained work in the cotton fields, but he set his sights on bigger things. He wondered what it would be like to rob a train.

In 1914 Willis Newton found himself in Cisco, Texas. In need of a job, he again found work in the cotton fields. There, he ran into an old friend named Red Johnson, whom he had known for fifteen years. Between his wages from picking cotton and what he made from gambling, Willis had accumulated $85. Feeling flush, he and Johnson quit the cotton fields and hung around town playing poker and shooting dice. By the time two weeks had passed both men were out of money. While wondering what to do next, Willis suggested to Johnson that they rob a train.

CLINE, TEXAS

From Cisco, Texas, Willis Newton and Red Johnson made their way to the small town of Sabinal. Willis carried a Colt .45 single-action revolver, a weapon he had acquired for $10 several months earlier in Fort Worth. While in Sabinal, the two men were wandering around the town's wagon yard when Johnson spotted a .30-.30 Winchester rifle laying in the back of a wagon. Johnson grabbed it and the two ran away. Now, both men were armed.

From Sabinal, they traveled to Uvalde, twenty-two miles to the southwest. Once in town, Willis decided that he too wanted a Winchester rifle. One night he and Johnson kicked in the door of a store and took a brand new .30-.30 along with several boxes of shells. This done, they walked to the railroad depot where the westbound Southern Pacific passenger train traveling on the Galveston, Harrisburg & San Antonio Railway had pulled into the station. Newton knew that after the train departed Uvalde, it traveled to the station at Cline, twenty-two miles to the west. Newton decided to rob the train when it stopped at Cline to take on water.

Willis learned that the train would depart at 11 p.m., but then he discovered that the shells he had taken would not fit the Winchester. He and Johnson raced back to the store, broke in again, and exchanged the shells for the correct ones. By the time they returned to the station, the train had departed.

Willis remained convinced that Cline would be the ideal location to rob the train, so having no other means of travel, they set out on foot. Their intention was to wait for the next westbound Southern Pacific to pull into the Cline station where they would board it and rob it.

The weather was cold. Newton and Johnson both wore heavy black overcoats and slept out in the open. Along the way, they burglarized a house where Red obtained a newer pair of boots. Three days later, on the afternoon of December 30, 1914, they arrived at the Cline station and learned that the train stopped at 11:30 p.m. The two men waited behind the shadows of the freight house.

Right on time, the Southern Pacific pulled into the station. As the locomotive idled, one of the train crew added water to the boiler from a large tank nearby. The engineer, along with another crewman, busied himself with performing the routine inspection and maintenance required at such stops. Though the train did not linger long at these remote stations, passengers were free to exit the car and stroll around the premises for a few minutes.

When the engineer signaled that the time to depart was approaching, the handful of passengers taking a break on the station dock ambled back into the cars.

In hiding, Newton and Johnson pulled the linings out of their overcoats to fashion masks.

Moments later as the train was preparing to pull away from the station, Newton and Johnson emerged from the shadows and climbed aboard the rear sleeping car. They were confronted by the brakeman, who immediately ordered them off the train, but when Newton jammed his revolver into the man's belly he offered no more resistance.

The two fledgling outlaws located the porter and, at gunpoint, ordered him to awaken the passengers. As soon as the travelers left their berths and stood in the hallway, they were approached by the bandits who demanded their money and valuables. The frightened passengers complied. One of the first to be robbed was a man named Watkins, who turned out to be the superintendent of the Southern Pacific Railroad.

All of the men were robbed. If a man and woman were together, both were robbed, but single women were left alone. The robbery took place in a matter of a few minutes and the passengers were sent back to their berths. Hours later when the train stopped at Spofford in the southern part of Kinney County, the two robbers jumped off and fled on foot from the scene.

Newton and Johnson had missed an opportunity to harvest even more money from the passengers. During the robbery, they ignored the private drawing rooms of the sleeper cars. It was reported that one of them was occupied by a wealthy Mexican citizen who was traveling with over $10,000 in money and $15,000 worth of jewelry. The robbers escaped with just over $4,700.

After leaving the train, the two robbers made their way to Crystal City, forty miles to the southeast where Willis's mother lived. If an organized search for and pursuit of the robbers was ever undertaken, there is no record of it, and their identities remained a complete mystery for another half-century. For years, searches for specific details relating to the Cline, Texas, train robbery, other than the identity of the first man robbed, led to dead ends. Newspaper reportage of the crime was spotty and incomplete, and a search of the records of the Southern Pacific Railroad Company yielded no information whatsoever.

What little is known about the Cline train robbery of 1921 came from Willis Newton himself over a half-century later. During an interview, he admitted his role in the affair, identified his partner as Red Johnson, and stated that it was his first train robbery.

Willis Newton went on to enjoy an amazing and successful career as a bank and train robber. For the first few years, his gang consisted of individuals who came and went, but in time he recruited his brothers—Jess,

Doc, and Joe—along with Brentwood Glasscock. With Willis as the leader and planner, the gang was also responsible for the successful robberies of eighty banks. Most of the bank robberies were in Texas and Colorado, with some as far east as Arkansas and as far north as Canada. Following the successful Cline, Texas, train robbery, Willis engineered another five.

BELLS, TEXAS

In 1921, Bells, Texas, was a tiny community located fifteen miles south of Denison. Imbued with the notion that robbing trains was a lucrative profession, Willis Newton began to focus on this location for his next heist.

By the spring of 1921, three of Willis's brothers and Glasscock had become regular members of the gang. Glasscock had been a member of the gang previously, left, and then came back. According to Willis, Glasscock, ". . . wasn't fit for nothing, just only to drive the car. He knowed all about a car and was a good driver."[1]

The Wild West days of employing horses for train holdups and escapes was long past. Willis was partial to Studebakers and began using them regularly for his robberies, both bank and train. He preferred the Studebaker "Big Six" and the "Special Six." Willis claimed they were the best road cars of the day, that they were "tough," and that "you could just run them into anything."[2] Invariably, the Studebakers used by the gang were stolen ones. They would be driven until the tread on the tires was worn down, discarded, and new ones appropriated.

Accompanied by brother Jess and Glasscock, Willis traveled from where they were living at the time in Tulsa, Oklahoma, down to Glenwood, Texas, where there was a transfer station for the Katy Railroad. As they watched from hiding, the gang members observed several large sacks being lifted into the mail car. The sacks were made of heavy canvas, and when filled they assumed a square shape and were secured at the top with a big brass lock. These were the types of sacks used by the Federal Reserve and other banks to ship currency. Willis discovered that similar sacks were loaded into a mail car every night. He assumed they all contained a lot of money.

Willis also learned that the train stopped at the small town of Bells, Texas. The three men traveled to that location. Willis explained that he and Glasscock would enter the mail car and, after the train had traveled a short distance, would throw the mailbags out. When the train slowed down on arriving at Denton, Willis and Glasscock would jump from it and make their way back down the tracks to the loot where they would be met by Jess in one of the Studebakers.

On the night of the robbery—August 25, 1921—the weather was warm and the doors to the mail car left open. As the train pulled out, Willis and Glasscock ran out of hiding and jumped into the opening. The two were immediately confronted by the mail clerk who reached for his revolver. He wasn't fast enough and before he could pull his weapon from the holster Willis had his own weapon out and pointed at the man's chest. As he took the clerk's weapon away, Willis noticed a second clerk lurking in the shadows and in the process of drawing his handgun. Willis quickly disarmed him and made the two men lie face down on the floor of the car. Yet a third clerk made his presence known, and a moment later was lying next to the others.

At that point, Willis noted that Glasscock had withdrawn to the opening of the mail car, afraid to come deeper inside. He ordered his accomplice to come inside the mail car, where upon seeing the three clerks disarmed and lying on the floor, Glasscock's courage returned and he began acting tough, striking the defenseless clerks. Years later when interviewed, Willis referred to Glasscock as a "dirty louse" and a "dirty coward."

Somehow Willis got the train stopped, and when he did, he and Glasscock threw the sacks onto the ground and jumped down after them. The train resumed its journey to Denton, while the two outlaws waited for brother Jess to arrive in the Studebaker. The sacks were loaded into the trunk, and moments later the robbers made their escape. Later, when they stopped long enough to open the sacks and count the money, they discovered they only came away with a few thousand dollars. Willis later learned that this was a smaller, secondary shipment of currency and that the larger one had occurred the day before.

What has been referred to as the Bells, Texas, train robbery received very little attention, and coverage by newspapers was light and spare of facts. Because the amount of money stolen was relatively small, and because the identity of the robbers was not known or even suspected, the matter was soon dropped.

As with the Cline, Texas, train robbery of December 30, 1914, specific details of the Bells robbery eluded investigators until Willis Newton was interviewed during the 1970s, wherein he revealed who was involved and the *modus operandi*. By then, Willis and his brothers were old men, had spent considerable time in prison, and had either served their appropriate sentences or outlived the statute of limitations for all their train and bank robberies.

BLOOMBERG, TEXAS

Disappointed with the amount of money taken from the Bells, Texas, robbery, Willis wasted no time in planning another heist. While hiding out in Texarkana, Texas, the gang would walk down to the depot every day and scrutinize the activity there. They noticed once each week when the train arrived from Shreveport, a man would climb out of the express car carrying a big black box, which he deposited at the express office. Willis discovered that the black box contained currency.

The outlaw studied the situation, and in the process learned the route of the Shreveport train. In the end, he decided the greatest potential for stealing the big black box full of money would be when the train stopped at Bloomberg, Texas, twenty miles to the south.

Willis, Doc, and Jess Newton, along with Brent Glasscock, traveled to Bloomberg, located the train station, and found a convenient hiding place in the nearby woods. After determining the location where they would halt the train and rob it, they made arrangements for brother Joe to pick them up.

The Newton brothers and Glasscock watched from their hiding spot as the train took on water and conducted the necessary inspections. The passengers lolled around the platform visiting and smoking. It was 10 p.m. on September 6, 1921. Moments later when all was ready, the conductor gave the signal to depart. Just as the train pulled away from the Bloomberg station, the four robbers ran from their place of concealment and jumped onto the blinds.

As the train approached the Sulphur River Bridge ten miles to the north, Willis and Jess made their way over the tops of the cars and the tender and into the locomotive cab where they waved their revolvers at the engineer and fireman. Once he had their attention, Willis told the engineer to start slowing down as the train approached the bridge. He further instructed the frightened man to stop the train when the mail car was just off the north side of the bridge and the rest of the cars remained on the structure.

Willis climbed back on top and ran back to the mail car. Near the middle of the car was a vent that had been cranked open to get fresh air into it. Willis pulled a bottle of formaldehyde from his pocket, uncorked it, and dumped the contents into the car. At the same time, he yelled into the opening that it was poison and ordered the clerks to slide open the car door. The smell of the formaldehyde frightened the clerks and they rushed to open the doors and scramble out of the car.

Willis located a porter and ordered him to uncouple the mail car from the trailing ones. This done, he ordered the porter into the mail car and asked him about the location of the big black box. The man explained that the box was not on the car this night. Disappointed at this failure, Willis hunted throughout the express car and found three sacks of registered mail.

Willis returned to the locomotive and ordered the engineer to pull the train forward, leaving the passenger coaches behind on the bridge. Later, on arriving at Texarkana, the gang of robbers took the mail sacks, left the train, and told the engineer to head back to the Sulphur River bridge and hook up the cars that had been left there. This done, the gang ran into the woods to a predetermined location where they were picked up by brother Joe.

According to Willis Newton, after opening the mail sacks all they found was "a bunch of bonds and stuff," some of which was converted into money.

As with the Cline and Bells, Texas, train robberies, information on this episode was scarce until Willis Newton revealed the details of the heist during the 1970s.

PAXTON, ILLINOIS

Less than a week after the Texarkana train robbery, the Newton Gang traveled to Paxton, Illinois, and made plans to hold up an Illinois Central passenger train No. 3. Paxton was a small town located one hundred miles south of Chicago. As with the gang's bank robberies, their train heists had fallen into a loose routine, a pattern, which for Willis proved to be successful. If something was working, Willis must have seen no reason to change. He expected the robbery of the Illinois Central to proceed smoothly with the expected results. He was not prepared for what was to follow.

According to Willis, he and Jess planned to board the Illinois Central "at the junction"[3] and ride it for twenty miles before ordering the engineer to pull to a stop on a bridge. Joe, Doc, and another man were to wait for them in the getaway car at a location three hundred yards from the bridge. It is not clear who the other man was, as Willis seldom mentioned sometime partner Glasscock by name. The other man, according to Willis, was used occasionally "because he was a pretty good driver."

On November 8, 1921, after climbing across the top of the coal tender, Willis and Jess dropped into the cab of the locomotive, pointed revolvers at Jack Fogarty, the engineer, and instructed him to stop the train at the prescribed location, a bridge a few miles down the line. There, he was to pull the engine, tender, and mail car off the bridge but leave the passenger coaches perched on the structure so that no one could get out. He then ordered Fogarty to uncouple the engine, tender, express, and mail cars from the rest of the train and move a short distance down the track. After warning the engineer and fireman to remain near the locomotive, Willis and Jess walked back to the mail car. Willis pounded on the door and demanded the postal clerk open it. When he received no response, he knocked on the windows, but still heard nothing. By this time, the engineer walked up and apparently interested in getting all the passengers and mail clerks safely to Chicago, offered to assist in getting into the car and bringing out the mail.

Grudgingly, the mail clerk, Ed Reef, opened the door slightly and admitted the engineer. Once in, however, neither the engineer nor the clerk would respond to Willis's demands. Frustrated at the delay and annoyed that the employees were not doing what they were told, Willis reached into the axle box and withdrew a handful of grease. He lit it, and as it began to burn, threw it into the mail car. Within seconds, the blob of grease was burning furiously and filling the car with acrid smoke. It wasn't long until the men inside shouted that they were coming out.

Willis called for them to remain where they were, that if they stepped out of the door he would shoot them. He could hear them coughing and otherwise reacting to the toxic fumes. After he determined that they had been sufficiently punished, he allowed them to come out, and he ordered, "Bring everything with you."

Willis stated that "All they brought out was just two or three small sacks of mail and the damned old mail clerk would not come out."[4] Unable to endure the smoke any longer, however, the clerk finally relented and climbed out of the car. In his interviews, Willis said, "When he finally did, I said something to him, and he pushed me. I reared back and slapped him."

As Willis and the mail clerk were engaged in their confrontation, two things happened that didn't go according to the script Willis had established. For one, the mail car had caught fire from the burning grease. For another, contrary to what Willis intended, several passengers, along with conductor Frank M. Williams, had climbed out of the cars and were watching the goings-on.

According to the next day's issue of the *Carbondale Free Press*, several of the passengers were soldiers, were armed, and "were anxious to shoot, but the clerks were placed in front of the looters for protection." One of the passengers had a shotgun and fired it at the robbers. Willis said, "That old shotgun didn't bother me."[5] In spite of Willis's claim that he was not bothered, he and Jess picked up the mail sacks and ran as fast as they could to the getaway car. On reaching it, they drove away, this time heading to Terre Haute, Indiana. On the way, Willis opened the mail sack and counted the take. "We only got a few hundred dollars and a few thousand dollars in bonds. A puny pisspot of money for all the hell we went through."[6] According to Chief Postal Inspector A. H. Germer, the robbers got away with a total of $400.00 and overlooked a mail pouch containing another $100,000.

During the robbery, several people who were driving along the highway near the railroad tracks claimed they heard shooting and, on arriving in Paxton, alerted the county sheriff. In a short time, a posse consisting of both lawmen and citizens hurried to the scene of the robbery, arriving long after the robbers had escaped.

As with previous robbery escapades, Willis's account did not match the details reported in area newspapers. The November 8, 1921, issue of the *Carbondale Free Press* stated that, "Few robberies in the annals of outlaw history compare in the viciousness with the mail robbery . . . when seven masked men held up the Illinois Central passenger train No. 3 four miles south of Paxton." The report stated that the robbers hurled "incendiary bombs" through "a bullet shattered door." The mail car was destroyed by the fire, "reduced to ashes all but the steel hull of the coach." One report stated that the mail car had been "dynamited." Another said that two charges of dynamite had been used.

Despite Willis's claim that no harm ever befell his robbery victims, the newspaper reported that: "During the robbery, the robbers abused the clerks with revolvers by hitting them over the head, three more or less being seriously injured.

"J. Barrett . . . was struck with a revolver and fell down a 12-foot embankment. Tom Baker, Negro, was hit over the head, cutting the scalp severely and necessitating several stiches. Ben Bovinett also suffered a blow and a laceration of the scalp. The colored porter on the train was shot."

The newspaper report also stated that the engineer was forced at gunpoint to "induce the mail clerks to open the mail car doors." It also related that after taking what they wanted, they "made bonfires of the mail."

The November 8 issue of the *Edwardsville Intelligencer* reported that the posses searching for the train robbers "numbered more than 500 deputy sheriffs, railroad detectives, and other volunteers." Arthur Moon, the porter reported shot by one of the robbers, "has two bullet wounds in his body and may die."

The *Intelligencer* also reported that: "The fireman, W. H. Bangs, was shot three times; Thomas Barker was slugged and beaten; passenger J. H. Knowlton wounded by bullets; and unidentified baggage clerk wounded by bullets."

On November 9, the *Carbondale Free Press* reported that Arthur Moon, the porter, died at a hospital in Champaign, Illinois, from gunshot wounds.

At every opportunity, Willis read newspaper accounts of his robberies, so there is little doubt that he was aware of the reporting of his aggressive and murderous behavior related to the Paxton train robbery. In spite of that, during the interviews he provided decades later, he never mentioned such behavior or any of its consequences, preferring instead to portray himself as a Robin Hood type of character who thwarted the goals and ambitions of the powerful and what he regarded as corrupt organizations such as railroads and banks.

In truth, the Paxton train robbery was not the only time the Newton Gang employed firearms against their victims.

ST. JOSEPH, MISSOURI

Almost a year had passed since the Newton Gang's last train robbery, and Willis was itching to try another. Weeks earlier, he learned from the late Des Moines Billy, a small-time gangster, that on certain nights of the week at 11 p.m., a $40,000 packing house payroll would arrive on the Chicago, Burlington, and Quincy freight at Union Train Yard in St. Joseph, Missouri, located fifty miles north of Kansas City. The train, which was on a route from Kansas City to Omaha, stopped two tracks away from the main depot where there was very little light. On the night of December 8, 1922, with Joe driving, the gang arrived at a point near the depot and stopped. After observing the goings-on for nearly an hour while they waited for the targeted train to arrive, they left the automobile, crept into the train yard, and took up a position near where the express car would be parked. Other than the robbers, there was no one about.

A few minutes later, the train arrived. Within moments after pulling to a stop, the engineer and fireman climbed down from the cab and undertook their routine inspection and maintenance. At the same time, the mail clerk, R. V. Ott, was transporting registered sacks and mail sacks from the Chicago, Burlington, and Quincy train No. 23 to the newly arrived express car. As he approached the car, Ott was confronted by four men pointing three revolvers and one shotgun at him. They ordered him to drop the bags to the ground. Eager to harvest some newfound riches, the Newtons snatched up the sacks and raced across the deserted portion of the train yard and back toward their getaway car.

After speeding away from the yard, the gang stopped several miles away and opened the sacks, eager to count their ill-gotten gains. Much to their surprise and dismay, the sacks contained no cash whatsoever; the only things of value they found were some Liberty bonds. Willis learned later that the $40,000 payroll they had designs on had arrived the previous evening. Des Moines Billy's information had been erroneous.

Years later when Joe Newton spoke about the St. Joseph robbery, he said: "When I think about it now, I see we didn't have any sense. Any of us. We didn't have any masks on either. But people like [the mail clerk], they're excited and they can't recognize you later. Anyway, they didn't have any pictures of us. There wasn't no such thing as the FBI. That was before the FBI."

The following morning's issue of the *Joplin Globe* reported that the robbers got away with only one registered sack along with five sacks of first-class mail. St. Joseph police Captain Kelly stated that he "now has all available officers and men scouring the eastern part of the city for traces of the bandits." They found none.

Coincidentally, at the same time the Newton Gang was holding up the St. Joseph train, another gang of robbers made away with $2,500 stolen from a train while it was stopped at the depot at Kansas City. The four men were arrested a short time later, but the money was never recovered.

Following the robbery, the Newton Gang traveled to Kansas City and checked into a hotel. Here, they knew a fence that would give them ninety cents on the dollar for the bonds. By the time the deal was finalized, according to Willis, they "only got a couple thousand dollars. . . ."

Low on money and having just come from a less than successful robbery, Willis cast about for another target for the Newton Gang.

Willis was still convinced that the best chance for making a huge score was with train robberies. The last few attempts, however, had failed to produce much in the way of wealth. But instead of being discouraged, Willis continued to plot and scheme, looking forward to the day when his dream of harvesting a great sum of money from a train would come true. It was not long in coming.

According to Joe Newton, the gang attempted to rob an Illinois Central train a few weeks after the St. Joseph holdup. He was unable to remember exactly where or when it transpired. For this robbery attempt, the gang departed somewhat from their normal routine and carried a few sticks of dynamite with them.

On approaching the express car that they had identified as their target, the gang noticed the door had been fastened from the inside and would not yield to their attempts to open it. The mail clerks were inside but refused to open the door. Willis said: "So we got the dynamite and cut it off so that it was about like a big fire cracker . . . and we throwed [it] back in there [through a window]. It wouldn't have hurt them. We didn't want to hurt anybody. So we'd throw it in there and it'd be spewing, and they'd run to the other end of the car. Then it'd go off, 'boom!' Then we'd throw one in the other end and they'd run this way and it'd go off, 'boom!'"[7]

Jess decided to grab some greasy rags he found in the axle box, light them, and toss them into the car in the hopes that the smoke would force the mail clerks to open the door to obtain some fresh air. Unfortunately, the burning rags set the car on fire. As smoke billowed out of the car's windows, the clerks opened the door and jumped out. By this time, however, the express car was burning so furiously that it was impossible for the robbers to enter it. Foiled, Willis led them away.

When the gang was several miles from the scene, one of them looked out the back window and could see the blaze. Joe said, "We could see that fire for a long way."

RONDOUT, ILLINOIS

It has been called the greatest train robbery in the history of North America. It involved one of the most effective and efficient outlaw gangs ever to practice their trade in the United States, one led by a fearless man who remained out of the headlines for decades and far from the notice of law enforcement. Save for only a handful of his peers in the robbery business, no one knew of the phenomenal successes and intricate details relative to the Newton Gang until half a century later, when the leader consented to a series of interviews.

In addition to the Newton Gang, the Rondout train robbery also involved Chicago politicians and government officials, all of whom saw an opportunity to get rich. The robbery had all the elements of a thriller, a fast-paced movie: a daring holdup and shooting followed by a pursuit and capture. And Willis Newton was in the middle of it all.

During the spring of 1924, Willis Newton and his brothers Joe, Jess, and Doc, checked into a first-class hotel in Chicago. Content with Willis as leader, the mastermind who planned all the details of the train and bank robberies, Joe, Jess, and Doc entertained themselves by visiting nightclubs, attending Chicago Cubs baseball games, and otherwise spending the money from an earlier San Marcos, Texas, bank robbery. Meanwhile, Willis was doing his homework lining up contacts to facilitate the next big robbery. One of the contacts was a local politician named Big Jim Murray.

During an interview in the 1970s, Willis said: "First off, let me tell you Tulsa and Chicago are crooked towns; they are now and they always have been. It don't matter—crooks, cops, bankers, or politicians—they're all as crooked. It's just a matter of who is paying who and how much."

Big Jim Murray, in addition to being an elected politician, made most of his money as a bootlegger—running beer from outside Chicago to the speakeasies. A speakeasy was a place that sold illegal alcoholic drink during the Prohibition years (1920–1933). Though millions of dollars were spent to enforce the Prohibition-related laws, the efforts proved impossible, in large part because political figures, government employees, and law enforcement personnel all cashed in on the opportunities presented by selling illegal drink.

As a result of his political position, Murray received inside information about Chicago mail shipments arriving and leaving via trains. Almost daily, shipments of $1 million to $3 million departed Chicago for banking institutions in the east. Murray was provided this information by US Postal Inspector William James Fahy. In exchange for schedules, as well as the kinds and exact amounts of money being shipped by registered mail on the trains, Murray provided Fahy with prostitutes and inside information on racehorses. Before realizing it, Fahy was completely in Murray's debt.

Murray had the knowledge. To take advantage of it, he needed an effective, professional gang, one experienced in train robbery from the planning aspect to the ultimate escape and division of money. Enter Willis Newton.

Murray met with Willis and explained what he had in mind. After listening to Murray go over the specifics of the mail and money shipments, as well as the railroad schedules and other logistics, Willis grew enthusiastic. The robbery of a Chicago, Milwaukee & St. Paul train, given all the pertinent information, could be executed without a hitch and escape would be optimized.

Willis liked Murray's idea. He also pointed out that the Newton Gang was unknown to the Chicago police and other Illinois law enforcement authorities. When Murray informed Willis that the haul from a heist such as this could yield as much as $3 million, Willis readily agreed. For months now, Willis had visions of making a big haul so he could retire from train and bank robbery and settle down permanently in Uvalde, Texas, where he and his brothers would live like royalty.

Initially, brother Joe, who rarely went against Willis, was opposed to the robbery, insisting that with that much money involved, along with robbing the mail being a federal crime, it would place intense pressure on law enforcement to mount an aggressive pursuit. With the large rewards that would undoubtedly be offered, Joe maintained, the chances were excellent that someone would tip off the police. Joe, however, was outvoted. During an interview in 1973, Joe said he was against robbing the train "because everybody who ever tried such a big robbery got caught some way or the other."

As the plan was developing, one of Murray's men took Willis to the Chicago train yard to show him the layout. From a vantage point, the two men observed "six or seven trucks pull up to deliver the registered mail sacks."[8] It was suggested to Willis that they pull the holdup while the sacks were being unloaded from the trucks and before they were carried to the train. Willis didn't care for the idea; he did not like the location, there were too many people around, and he was concerned there might be some shooting. Willis was an experienced train robber, and he explained that a successful heist has a greater chance of success if it is undertaken after the train had pulled away from the station and made to stop at a relatively remote location. Murray's henchman was not keen on Willis's idea. Willis thought Murray's partner was a fool and a coward, but he told him he would take some time to think about the proposition for a while and get back to him.

Willis continued to do his homework. He met with his gang members and together they decided they were going to learn more about the schedule and route of the train carrying the registered mail sacks. For the next two months Willis and the gang studied these matters as well as others, including movements of the police and other logistical concerns.

For the job, Willis recruited former partners Brent Glasscock and Herbert Holliday. The plan was to stop the CM&SP train outside of Rondout, Illinois, a small community located forty miles north of downtown Chicago. Near the place where the train was to be stopped, two Cadillacs would be parked to be employed as getaway vehicles. After the train was pulled to a stop, the gang would enter the mail car, unload the registered mail sacks, and place them in the Cadillacs. From Rondout, the gang would then drive to a body and paint shop just outside the city limits of Chicago that happened to be owned by Murray's uncle. There, the gang would rendezvous with Murray, split the take, and drive away. Willis explained to Murray and his henchman that this was the best way to rob the train, and if they didn't agree to Willis's plan, they needed to find another gang to pull the heist. Murray consented.

With the plan firmed up, all that was needed was exact information as to the precise timing of the next multimillion-dollar shipment, information that would be provided by postal inspector Fahy. While they were waiting, Willis sent his wife, Louise, to Wisconsin to stay with her mother. He did not tell her anything about the plans to rob the train.

While Willis and the gang were waiting for the timing of the robbery to fall into place, Big Jim Murray's henchman reappeared. He informed Willis that once each week, a $40,000 payroll distributed throughout three sacks departed Chicago for Cicero, Indiana. The train left early in the morning, and the truck delivering the payroll from the post office to the mail car carried only one man—the driver. Murray wanted the gang to rob the truck. Willis considered that this might be a way Murray wanted to test the efficiency of the gang. He also thought it might prove to be an easy score. He agreed to do it.

Once again, Joe pointed out the potential hazards and risks of such a robbery. He noted that there was a police station two blocks away, and just two tracks over, pedestrians were walking around. Willis attempted to calm Joe by telling him they would be gone before anyone would be able to do anything.

On the morning of the holdup, the gang arrived at the rail yard in a Cadillac and parked where they could not be seen but where they could observe the goings-on. Presently, the truck carrying the payroll rolled into the yard. Joe, who was driving, pulled the Cadillac in front of the truck, blocking passage to the mail car. The gang exited the vehicle, each man carrying a weapon, every one of them pointed at the truck driver, who raised his hands in immediate surrender.

Joe, carrying bolt cutters, went to the rear of the truck and cut the locks off. Another gang member climbed into the truck and tossed out the three payroll sacks along with seven other bags of registered mail. The sacks were loaded into the Cadillac and, leaving the stunned truck driver still sitting in his cab with his hands raised, the gang raced away.

After driving fifty miles south of Chicago, the gang pulled off the highway onto a dirt road and stopped at a somewhat remote location. There were no houses or anything else to suggest that someone might show up. There, they opened the sacks and counted a total of $35,000 in cash. Willis counted out seven piles of $5,000 each: a share for each gang member and a $5,000 share for Murray to split with Postal Inspector Fahy who had initially provided information about the shipment.

A few days later, information reached Willis from Murray of a large shipment of cash set to leave on the Chicago, Milwaukee & St. Paul train. Willis alerted the gang and together they began to fit the logistical pieces together. One of the first orders of business was to acquire two Cadillacs. Normally, the Newton Gang employed the large Studebaker Sixes or Eights or Buick Sixes in their holdups, but the new Cadillacs provided sufficient power and speed, and were roomy enough to carry the gang members, along with the sacks of stolen money and mail.

Two of the gang members stole two brand new 1924 Cadillac touring cars, one a seven-passenger, the other a five-passenger. The cars were hidden in a garage until it was time to put them to use.

On June 11, 1924, Willis called a meeting with the gang where he laid out the specific plans for the train robbery. Joe, Doc, and Glasscock were to retrieve the Cadillacs and park them near Buckley Crossing outside of the small town of Rondout, the exact location where the train would be stopped. They left for Rondout early the next morning. That evening, Willis and Holliday, dressed in overalls and caps similar to what the engineer and fireman wore, were driven to the train station where the CM&SP was preparing to pull out. Just as the engineer signaled he was ready to depart, Willis and Holliday ran from their hiding place and jumped onto the blind of a car closest to the engine. It happened to be the mail car in which the registered mail was being transported.

On reaching the blind, Willis found half a dozen hobos already seated there. They thought Willis and Holliday were lawmen come to roust them. Playing the role, Willis pulled his revolver from a pocket and ordered the hobos off the train.

After leaving the station, the train picked up speed and was soon roaring through the countryside. As the train approached Buckley Crossing, the engineer blew the whistle, the usual warning to any travelers who might be approaching the intersection. This was the signal Willis was waiting for.

From the blind, Willis and Holliday climbed atop the mail car, made their way across the top to the coal tender, and then dropped into the locomotive cab. There, he and Holliday pointed revolvers at the engineer and fireman. Both men, clearly frightened, raised their hands and began begging the strangers not to shoot them. Willis explained that they would not be harmed if they did what they were told. Willis then instructed the engineer, S. R. Waite, to pull the train to a stop at Buckley Crossing, which by now was less than two miles ahead. Too frightened to comply, the trembling engineer kept his hands raised and continue to plead for his life.

Irritated, Willis placed his revolver in a pocket, grabbed the engineer by the arm, and said, "You better get them damn hands on the throttle and stop this train or I'll blow your head off!"

Fearing for his life, the engineer turned his attention to the throttle. Since he took so long to respond to Willis's commands, the engineer pulled the train to a stop well past the location that had been selected. Willis instructed him to back the train up and place the mail car right on the crossing.

As this back and forth between Willis and the engineer was going on, the fireman, R. J. Biddle, begged Holliday, "Mister, don't point that gun at me. I'm scared to death." Holliday responded, "By God, brother, you ain't any worse scared than I am."[9]

When the train finally pulled to a stop, Willis ordered everyone out of the locomotive cab. He instructed Doc, who had been waiting at the crossing, to "go over to the other side of the train from where we were [and] unload the sacks and watch for anyone sneaking out of the train on that side." Joe and Glasscock were told to walk down the tracks alongside the train and look for guards.

Glasscock crossed to the other side of the tracks where Doc was. Joe arrived at the caboose where he found the brakeman and conductor. The brakeman was climbing down when Joe raised his shotgun and pointed it at him. Seeing this, the conductor remained in the doorway. The brakeman told Joe he needed to walk back down the track and flag down any oncoming train. Joe assumed the man was lying and was concocting an excuse to get away from the trouble. Joe wasn't concerned, for there was little but empty space between Rondout and Buckley Crossing.

Joe ordered the conductor, an old man, to climb down. The conductor told Joe it was too cold outside and he wasn't going to come out until he got his coat. Joe asked him where his coat was and the conductor pointed to a large box with a lid. As the conductor reached to lift the lid, Joe, fearing he might be reaching for a weapon, ordered him to stop or he would be shot. The conductor ignored Joe, opened the lid to the box, and withdrew a heavy coat from the interior.

After the engine was uncoupled from the rest of the train, the conductor, along with the engineer, was escorted by Willis and Jess to the mail car. Willis looked around to discern the positions of the rest of the gang. He spotted everyone but Glasscock. He inquired of Joe as to Glasscock's whereabouts and Joe replied that he had "run up ahead somewhere."[10]

Years later, Willis stated, "It was just like that bastard to not follow orders, but I didn't have time to chase after him." Instead, he told Joe to break the windows of the mail car. Joe smashed them in with the butt of his shotgun. (A subsequent newspaper report stated that the windows were shattered as a result of "a fusillade of bullets and rocks [crashing] through the window.) Willis asked Joe to hand him the bottle of formaldehyde he carried in his coat pocket.

Willis called to the mail clerks inside the car. He ordered them to open the door and come out or he would toss a container of "poison gas" into the car. There was no response from inside and the door did not move. Without a second warning, Willis threw the bottle through one of the windows. A few seconds later, the door slid open and Willis was surprised to find "sixteen or seventeen [mail clerks and guards] in there." He ordered the men carrying weapons to drop them on the floor of the car, climb out, and lay face down on the ground.

A somewhat different rendering of this part of the robbery was described by at least one reporter. This alternate version had Willis, carrying a bottle of formaldehyde in his pocket, climbing across the roof of the mail car, smashing the air vent at the top, and tossing the bottle in from that direction.

However it happened, Willis then ordered Joe and Holliday to collect all the weapons in the mail car and place them in one of the Cadillacs. This done, Willis put on a gas mask and climbed into the car, stood in the doorway looking down at the clerks and guards, and demanded to know which of them was the chief mail clerk. One of the captured men, Lewis Phillips, identified himself and Willis ordered him to put on another mask he produced and climb back into the car.

Willis, pointing his revolver at Phillips, told him he wanted all the registered mail sacks. Phillips said he could not tell one sack from another. Willis told Phillips that if he did not locate the registered mail sacks that he would kill him. The clerk went among the hundreds of mail sacks, finally retrieving sixty of them and bringing them to where Willis stood near the door. Willis instructed several more of the prone clerks outside to come to the door. He ordered the chief clerk to hand the sacks to the others who, in turn, were ordered to carry them to the waiting Cadillacs and stack them in the back seats and on the floorboards.

As the sacks were being loaded, the chief mail clerk called to Willis and asked him, "Is that your man that got shot out there?" Willis replied that nobody got shot. The clerk said that when he opened the door on the other side of the car, he watched as somebody shot a man.

Willis knew that Doc was stationed on the other side of the car. He went to the open door, looked out, and called out to Doc. He couldn't see him, but he heard someone moaning as if they were in pain. He recognized Doc's voice. Willis yelled at Joe and Holliday that Doc was injured and to go get him. As Holliday crawled under the mail car to reach the other side, someone took a shot at him. Willis realized it had been Glasscock doing the shooting.

Willis shouted at Glasscock to get over to the mail car immediately. When he arrived, he asked him if had shot Doc. Glasscock replied that he had not, that he "shot a Hoosier." Willis, anger rising, told Glasscock he had shot Doc. He then turned to the rest of the gang and ordered them to get Doc placed into one of the cars and have the clerks hurry up and finish loading the mail sacks, that it was time to get away. Doc was placed in the back seat of one of the vehicles atop a pile of mail sacks. When the loading was done, Willis ordered all the clerks to lie back down on the ground and remain there until they had driven away. It was one hour before dawn.

During the getaway, Willis was driving the lead car with Glasscock riding shotgun. After they had put thirty miles between themselves and the holdup site, Willis pulled to the side of the road to check on Doc, who had suffered several bullet wounds and was in great pain. He opened the rear door of the trailing Cadillac and looked in on his brother. Blood streamed from his wounds and soaked all the mail sacks. Before driving away, Willis instructed Joe to toss the handguns they had taken from the mail clerks into the nearby brush. He jumped back into the lead car and sped away to their predetermined rendezvous at the paint and body shop as fast as he could go.

After covering another fifty miles, Willis, ever the concerned brother, stopped again to check on Doc. Willis asked him if he needed some aspirin, that they would get some at the next town. Doc replied, "No, that might weaken my heart. I don't want no aspirin tablets."[11]

During the second stop, one of the mailbags somehow fell out of the trailing Cadillac. Because Willis was in a hurry and everyone was anxious to go into hiding before they were caught, no one noticed it. The following day, law enforcement authorities found the bag, and thus the escape route taken by the robbers.

An hour later, Willis led the gang into the paint and body shop. The first thing Willis did was check on Doc again. He was lifted from the backseat of the Cadillac and laid on the floor. One of the bullets had passed through his jaw and clipped off a piece of his tongue. Not long after they arrived, Big Jim Murray pulled into the garage.

Murray expressed concern, not so much about Doc, but about all the blood on the mail sacks. He thought Doc was going to die, and was worried that, one way or another, the police would learn about his death, piece all the evidence together, and come after him. Willis, still fuming, told Murray that if he didn't get a doctor to come and take care of Doc immediately, he was going to kill him. Joe, equally disturbed about his brother's wounds, echoed the threat. Murray agreed to get a doctor.

Glasscock and Holliday had no desire to wait around the paint and body shop while Doc's wounds were being tended to. They were both anxious to get as far away from Chicago as possible, the sooner the better. The two men argued for splitting up the money then and there and leaving the scene.

A division of the money took place. As soon as Glasscock, Holliday, and Jess pocketed their share, they decided to hurry out of town. Holliday departed within the hour. After hiding $40,000 of the money in a barn, Jess returned to Texas. Shares for Willis and Joe were given to Glasscock who was instructed to take them to Tulsa and leave them at the home of a relative where they would retrieve them later. Before departing Chicago, Glasscock also delivered $500,000 to Postal Inspector Fahy.

After Murray made a phone call, Willis and Joe transported Doc to a house owned by one of Murray's cohorts, a man named Walter McComb. According to Murray, a doctor would arrive in a short time. Doc was carried to a room on the second floor of the house. The doctor showed up a few minutes later. As Doc was being treated for his wounds, the morning edition of the June 12 *Decatur Daily Review* hit the streets with headlines screaming "$2,000,000 Loot Taken From Train." Newspaper headlines all across the country announced the train robbery. Even at that early date, it was already being reported as the largest haul from a train holdup in history.

An article in the *Bakersfield Morning Echo* reported a smaller amount of money taken in the robbery: "Mail Train Robbers Get 1 Million." Over the next few days, other newspaper articles mentioned amounts ranging from $500,000 to $3,000,000. The report, misinterpreting Glasscock's accidental shooting of Doc, stated, "The bandits and guards engaged in a pistol battle . . . and at least one of the robbers was reported shot." The report also stated that the robbers escaped in "four automobiles" after taking "40 pouches of registered mail containing bonds and currency from the Chicago Federal Reserve Bank and consigned to banks in the northeast."

The same article stated that "there was a crew of 70 mail clerks and guards on the train of eight cars [and that] they were all locked in and that in no event were they to open the doors. They were all armed and instructed to shoot to kill anyone attempting to force entrance into their car." It went on to say that the guards and clerks did no such thing and were forced out of the cars and lined up against the train.

While Willis went to check on the remaining stolen mailbags, Joe, along with Big Jim Murray, remained at the McComb residence with Doc.

On the morning of June 14, about two dozen policemen, acting on tips, arrived at McComb's residence, stormed the house, and arrested Joe, Doc, and Murray. The following morning, Willis arrived at the house to check on his brother. When he knocked on the door, it was thrown open and, according to Willis, "the place was crawling with policemen!"[12] Willis tried to put up a fight, but he was outnumbered and out-armed. He was placed in handcuffs. Later, the chief mail clerk of the Chicago, Milwaukee & St. Paul train who was forced to do Willis's bidding during the robbery was called in to identify him.

Doc was transferred to the county hospital where his wounds were treated. Joe was placed in the Chicago city jail. According to Joe, Police Captain William Schoemaker told him he was going to "whip the information out of him" and that he was "going to put him away for twenty-five years in the penitentiary."[13] Schoemaker made good his threats. The police captain beat Joe with his fists, breaking his nose, and then, "he tried to punch my eyes out."[14] Schoemaker was accompanied by a big Irish cop named Tapscott. Every time the captain beat on Joe, Tapscott wanted to step in and take a turn, but Schoemaker wouldn't let him. Joe said Tapscott would have killed him. The police beat Joe for seven straight days.

A number of the policemen left the house to focus on other aspects of the investigation, and three plainclothes cops remained to guard Willis. Once alone with his guards, Willis offered them $20,000 to let him go. After talking among themselves, the three officers agreed to accept the bribe. Wills explained he would have to call a woman he knew in Wisconsin and get her to withdraw the money from her bank account. The woman was, in fact, his wife, Louise, but he did not provide that information. The plan was for her to arrive the next evening on the train, hand the money over to the policemen, and he would be turned loose.

At 5 p.m. the next day as the policemen and Willis were preparing to drive to the depot to meet Louise, Police Captain Schoemaker arrived at the house. When Schoemaker inquired as to why they were preparing to leave, the three policemen revealed the arrangement they had made with Willis. Schoemaker said he wanted to be cut in on the deal.

At 6 p.m., Schoemaker, Willis, and the three policemen drove to the depot. Willis, along with two of the policemen, met Louise as she got off the train. Shoemaker and the third policeman watched from a distance. Without telling anyone that Louise was his wife, Willis said to her that he was in trouble, and that to get out of it he needed to pay $20,000 to his lawyers. He indicated the policemen. She assured him she could get the money, but she would have to go to a nearby bank and withdraw it from a safety deposit box. The plainclothesmen offered to escort them to the bank, and a moment later they, Willis, and Louise piled into a cab. Schoemaker and the other policeman followed behind.

At the bank, the cab waited outside while Louise went in and obtained the money—$20,000 in $1,000 bills. As she stepped out of the bank, Schoemaker drove up and took charge. Addressing the policemen, he said that Willis Newton was not to be released, that he was to be taken to jail. Schoemaker took possession of the money. Both Willis and Louise were transported to the city jail. Louise was dubbed "The Bandit Queen" by local newspapers.

Following a round of questions, Willis was placed in a cell at a jail in Wheaton, a small town on the outskirts of Chicago. Convinced that Louise was merely trying to do a favor and was not connected to the Rondout robbery, she was released.

According to an article in the June 14 edition of the *Murphysboro Daily Independent*, more than one dozen people had been arrested in connection with the train robbery. One of those arrested was a man named Paul Wage, an alias used by Joe Newton. Joe was found in possession of $1,500 in bills that had serial numbers corresponding to some that were stolen. The bills were described as "blood spattered."

The *Independent* also reported that Doc Newton, who was using the alias J. H. Wayne, was arrested and treated for three bullet wounds. He said he received them during an argument with a woman several days earlier. When Big Jim Murray was arrested, he gave his name as J. Mahoney.

The June 14 edition of the *Billings* [Montana] *Gazette* quoted a statement from government officials that they were confident "the holdup was the result of inside information obtained by someone connected with the post office or Federal Reserve banks" and that they were "conducting [an] investigation of this angle." Acting on tips, police were searching for Brent Glasscock, who was using the alias, Sam Grant, and Herbert Holliday who was going by the name Blackie Wilcox.

It was also learned that a federal warrant had been issued for the arrest of Louise Drafka (her maiden name) who, according to the June 30 issue of the *Decatur Daily Review,* "posed as the wife of Willis Newton and came from Milwaukee and obtained $36,000 to buy his release." (Willis never varied in his insistence that it was only $20,000.) In addition to being arrested in connection with the Rondout train robbery, the paper mentioned that Big Jim Murray "was served with a warrant charging him with mail robbery in connection with a million-dollar robbery three years ago in Union Station." Murray was released on bond.

Shortly after being arrested by the police, Willis was turned over to a panel of postal authorities for questioning. Among the panel members was US Postal Inspector William James Fahy, the man responsible for leaking pertinent information relating to the registered mail shipments to his coconspirator, Big Jim Murray. Fahy avoided the meetings, according to Willis, because he "knew I would rat him out."[15]

Willis decided on a plan. He told the panel that he was to meet Glasscock and Holliday in a saloon in St. Louis a couple of days hence. Willis suggested to the postal inspectors, "If you take me down there and let me go in and meet [them] . . . you can get them both. In truth, Willis was attempting to generate a conversation with Fahy so "I could get him to go along on the plan and let me get away in St. Louis. But I could never get to talk to Fahy alone."[16]

Willis, however, was taken to St. Louis. Willis claimed Fahy leaked word to the St. Louis newspapers that they were "bringing one of the train robbers down in order to capture other members of the gang."[17] Willis was afforded no opportunity to escape and was returned to the jail at Wheaton. A few weeks later, Willis was transferred to the jail at Rockford, sixty miles northwest of Chicago. On the day of the transfer, Fahy showed up with three inspectors to oversee the move. At first, Willis thought Fahy was going to arrange an escape for him, that the last thing that Fahy wanted was for Willis to get on the witness stand and implicate the postal inspector. As it turned out, Fahy was more inter-ested in putting Willis away for good. At Rockford, Willis was placed in solitary confinement. He was not allowed to see anyone and was not permitted newspapers or letters.

While Willis, Joe, and Doc were locked up, Jess was hiding in San Antonio and spending much of this time drinking whiskey and chasing women. When he was sober, Jess grew concerned about the large amount of robbery loot he was transporting in one of his suitcases. From time to time, he thought he should do something about it, perhaps hide it in a safe place where he could retrieve it later.

One day while Jess was in the middle of an extended drinking binge, he grabbed the suitcase full of money, hailed a cab, and headed out of San Antonio on the Old Fredericksburg Road. As they rode along, Jess shared his liquor with the cab driver, and after they had traveled several miles both men were drunk. At one point during the trip, Jess told the driver to stop. Jess climbed out of the cab, grabbed the suitcase, and walked out into the brush. When he was out of sight of the cab, he hid the suitcase under a large rock, staggered back to the cab, and the pair returned to San Antonio. (While testifying in court six months later, Jess stated he had placed the money in four glass jars at a location six miles from San Antonio.)

The following morning when Jess sobered up, he had only a vague recollection of hiding the money but could not remember exactly where. He hailed another cab and directed it back down the Old Fredericksburg Road to where he was convinced he had cached the money. Though he searched for over an hour, he was unable to locate it. For several days in a row, Jess traveled back to the general area where he stashed the suitcase, but never found it. As far as is known, this particular cache of Rondout train robbery money has never been found, and treasure hunters search for it to this day. A few days later, Jess crossed the border into Mexico and settled in at the border town of Villa Acuña located across the Rio Grande from Del Rio, Texas.

Somehow, federal authorities located Jess in Villa Acuña in the Mexican state of Coahuila. They sent undercover men to make Jess's acquaintance and determine if the money he was spending was some of the train robbery loot. They had no success, so they formulated another plan.

Over the years, Jess had developed a reputation as a top breaker of horses. His services were in demand on ranches in and around Uvalde. It was a reputation he took great pride in. If he wasn't making big money robbing trains and banks, Jess would have been quite happy working on ranches and breaking horses. The federal authorities learned of this information and decided to act on it.

The postal inspectors enlisted help from the Texas Rangers, who assigned Harrison Hamer to the case. Harrison was the brother of Frank Hamer who, at the time, was working as a Customs Agent. Frank would later go on to fame as one of the lawmen, a Texas Ranger, who ambushed the notorious bank robbers Bonnie Parker and Clyde Barrow, bringing their crime spree to an abrupt end.

Harrison Hamer, aware of Jess's reputation as a top horse breaker, developed a plan with the postal inspectors to get Jess on the north side of the Rio Grande where they could arrest him. One night in Villa Acuña, Mexico, Jess's new "friends" told him about a bronc across the river in Del Rio, Texas, that nobody was able to ride. They told Jess they were going to bet $500 that he could tame the horse and alternately begged and dared him to cross over to the north side of the river to ride him. Jess's pride and ego caused him to relax his caution, and he agreed to give it a try.

The next morning, Jess was observed by Hamer carrying his rigging across the border into Del Rio. After passing through the border inspection station, Jess proceeded toward an arena where the ride was to take place. An article about the legendary lawman in the March 21, 2005, issue of the *Floresville Chronicle Journal* related what happened next:

> As [Hamer] watched, he saw Jess come into the stands with his wife and another woman. He waited until Jess got up to leave the stands and he just passed near him he grabbed him by the arm and told him not to make a move and that he was under arrest. . . . Harrison then took Jess down below the grandstands and asked one of the cowboys

there to watch him. Harrison then went back and sent someone up in the grandstand to tell Jess's wife that Jess wanted her to come down for a moment, and as she passed by he also arrested her.

Jess was taken to a jail in San Antonio. He hired a team of lawyers and his case went back and forth for several months. In the end, he was extradited back to Chicago to stand trial with the others for the Rondout train robbery. In Chicago, Jess was interrogated by a team of detectives. He was told that if he cooperated and provided details of the train robbery and named names they would recommend he only be sentenced to one year in prison instead of the customary twenty-five. Jess agreed to cooperate and told them everything he knew.

While Jess was fighting extradition in Texas, other postal inspectors began to focus on William James Fahy, who by now had generated significant suspicion. Fahy enjoyed a stellar reputation as an effective agent among postal inspectors. In fact, he was once credited with solving a $338,000 depot robbery and sending crooked labor leader Tim Murphy to prison.

According to Willis in a later interview, "It was a woman that [eventually] tripped up Fahy." Willis explained that Fahy had arrested the woman's husband for mail robbery one year earlier. The woman was convinced that if she got close to Fahy, she could talk him into cutting a deal wherein her husband would be released from prison. One evening she got Fahy drunk, and he started bragging about his role in the Rondout train robbery. She reported to the postal inspectors and a short time later the investigation tightened around Fahy.

One of the first things the authorities did was tap Fahy's telephones. They were able to listen in on numerous conversations between the postal inspector and Big Jim Murray, who was still out on bond. A clandestine search of Fahy's files revealed that specific documents related to the Rondout robbery were missing.

At the same time, agents who were investigating Big Jim Murray were trying to devise a way in which they could catch him in possession of some of the stolen bonds. They enlisted another agent to serve as a plant, to represent himself to Murray as one who could convert stolen bonds into cash. At the time, it was nearly impossible for Murray to pass the bonds because their serial numbers had been provided to banks and other financial institutions. Chief Postal Inspector A. H. Germer told Fahy of the plot.

Fahy grew nervous on learning this information. If Murray were caught with the bonds, he might try to cut a deal for a lesser sentence by turning in his coconspirator. Before Fahy could regain his composure, he was told to attend a lunch meeting in a downtown Chicago hotel. As it turned out, the meeting was with a roomful of federal inspectors who interrogated Fahy for the rest of the day. Following the meeting, Fahy, as described by the August 27, 1924, issue of the *Waterloo Evening Courier*, as having bloodshot eyes and trembling hands as he was "escorted to his federal building desk where he slouched in his chair as US Deputy Marshals Howard and Carr placed him formally under arrest."

Fahy declared that he went along with Murray's plan to rob the train "in hopes of getting him myself. I tipped him off and told him he had better turn the bonds over to me. I wanted credit for the solution and recovery of the bonds. I was working as the 'lone wolf'. . . ."[18] Investigators were not swayed by Fahy's explanation.

Before October 1924 had ended, Herbert Holliday and Brent Glasscock were arrested. Glasscock and his wife, going by the aliases C. P. Reese and Ann Reese, had arrived in Battle Creek, Michigan, where they made inquiries relative to renting a room. Their whereabouts were discerned by a college student named Wayne Schaefer. Schaefer was standing in line at a Battle Creek post office and whiled away his time looking over the wanted posters tacked to a nearby bulletin board. One of the images was of a woman wearing a nurse's uniform. Convinced he knew who this woman was, he pulled down the wanted poster and asked to see the postmaster.

Schaefer was escorted to the postmaster's office where he explained that this same woman whose face was on the poster had arrived at a rooming house owned by his father and asked about renting one for her and her husband, whom she said was sick. The postmaster placed a call to postal inspectors who arrived minutes later.

Around midafternoon of the same day, Brent Glasscock arrived at the rooming house where he met his wife, who was waiting for him on the front porch. Glasscock was carrying a heavy suitcase. Together they went inside and paid in cash for the room for eight months. The couple then walked around to the side of the house and were about to climb the stairs to their room when two postal inspectors appeared and placed both under arrest. Inside the suitcase they found $80,000 in cash, money later identified as having come from the Rondout train robbery.

Glasscock caved under the pressure of interrogation. Up until this time, authorities had recovered some of the train robbery loot but felt Glasscock would be able to lead them to much more that was still missing. In a short time, Glasscock was confessing to his part in the robbery and providing details about other members of the gang. He promised to tell the police where they could find the rest of the money. He also provided important testimony relative to the deep involvement of Fahy.

In truth, Glasscock had never met Fahy, had never seen him. An inspector named Aldridge made the decision to get Glasscock on the witness stand to identify Fahy as the inside man on the train robbery. In exchange for this testimony, Aldridge told Glasscock, he would see that the prison sentences for the gang members would be reduced. Glasscock, who was facing twenty-five years to life in prison, would get a sentence of only five years if he cooperated. In spite of having never seen Fahy, Glasscock agreed.

During a subsequent hearing, Glasscock managed to get close enough to Willis to ask him which of the men in the courtroom was Fahy. Willis pointed him out. Later, when Glasscock was on the stand and he was asked to identify Fahy, he pointed straight at him with no hesitation. At the time, Fahy was sitting next to Big Jim Murray. The two men knew at that point that the game was over for them.

On November 8, 1924, the trial for all charged in the Rondout train robbery opened in the US District Court for Illinois, Judge Adam C.

Cliff presiding. Two hundred and fifty witnesses had been summoned to testify. Following the customary preliminaries, Benedict Short requested permission to approach the bench. Short was the attorney representing the Newton brothers as well as Brent Glasscock and Herbert Holliday. Short informed Judge Cliff that his clients wished to change their pleas from not guilty to guilty "on advice from counsel."[19] That left only Big Jim Murray and William Fahy to face a jury trial.

On November 16 and 17, Jess and Joe Newton were called to the witness stand. Joe provided details of the arrangements made with Murray to rob the registered mail sacks from the Chicago, Milwaukee & St. Paul train at Rondout, Illinois, and that Murray had received information of the shipment from a postal inspector. During the trial, it was established that Murray and Fahy were involved in most of the planning for the robbery and funneled information and directions to the Newton Gang, who had been recruited to pull off the heist.

Glasscock followed Joe Newton to the stand. He spent two hours relating details of meetings with Murray and Fahy in which a series of robberies were discussed. Glasscock stated that Murray was the actual brains behind the train robbery while Fahy provided information relative to "movements of large sums of money. . . ." Willis said, "Glasscock was lying his head off but his testimony nailed it for Murray and Fahy."[20]

While Glasscock was on the stand, attorneys questioned him about his shooting of Doc Newton and his "attempt to shoot Herbert Holliday."[21] They asked him if, by killing these two gang members, he intended to increase his share of the robbery loot. The *Wisconsin Rapids Daily Tribune* reported that Glasscock refused to answer the question on the grounds that it might incriminate him.

The same newspaper reported how Glasscock turned over nearly a half a million dollars in cash, bonds, and unsigned bills to the federal authorities. After explaining where he hid a portion of the robbery loot, Glasscock was escorted to Tulsa, Oklahoma, by five postal inspectors, the party arriving at the home of Chester Van Cleve, Glasscock's brother-in-law. When Van Cleve answered the knock on his door, Glasscock said, "Sorry to disturb you, but there is a lot of money hidden in your house and we want it."

Van Cleve, who knew nothing of the cache, was astonished. Glass-cock led the inspectors through the house, into a bedroom, and to a closet. He climbed onto a chair and, from a small hole in the ceiling of the constricted space, withdrew several wrapped packages of bonds and currency.

On November 25, Big Jim Murray and William Fahy were each sentenced to twenty-five years in prison for their roles in the Rondout train robbery. Fahy claimed he was innocent, that he had been framed. Judge Cliff ordered him transferred to the US Penitentiary in Atlanta, Georgia, to serve out his sentence.

As a result of pleading guilty and cooperating with the investigations of Murray and Fahy, Willis and his brothers were led to believe they would be sentenced to no more than five years in prison. Willis said later in an interview, "All of a sudden that old [postal inspector] Aldridge wanted to crawfish on what he promised me. He said [that instead], he was going to recommend that me and Doc get twelve years apiece, Joe for three years, and since Jess had cooperated so much he'd get a year." Their lawyer, Benedict Short, promised Willis he would go to Washington and work a deal with the attorney general to get the sentences that were promised. Short lived up to his word.

The Newton brothers, along with Brent Glasscock and Herbert Holliday, were readied for transfer to the federal prison at Leavenworth, Kansas. They were shipped by train to Kansas City where they were to board another that would take them to the prison.

Glasscock and Holliday had fallen out, were not getting along, and had threatened to kill each other during the ride from Chicago to Kansas City. The Newton brothers, who had been granted the light prison sentences they had initially been promised, were in high spirits.

By the end of 1924, most of the investigations into the Rondout train robbery had been completed and the principals all behind bars. During the months that had passed since the train robbery, more reports were issued by a variety of authorities claiming that the estimated total amount of cash, bonds, and notes stolen during the Rondout train robbery ranged from $1 million to $3 million, with most quoting the latter sum. It was also reported that while some of the money had been recovered, the majority of it was still missing. During interrogation, and during their time in court, none of the Newton brothers admitted to possessing any knowledge whatsoever of the whereabouts of the money.

On leaving Leavenworth, Willis Newton returned to Texas and his wife, Louise. There, he farmed until he passed away on August 22, 1979, at the age of ninety.

SOME TRAIN ROBBERY TERMINOLOGY

BLIND
The blind is a walkway between two passenger cars. This space was often covered with accordion-pleated leather or canvas. From the outside of the blinds to the outer edge of the cars was a space about twenty-four inches wide. A ladder ran from this space to the top of the car. Hobos would occasionally grab the ladder, climb a few rungs, and hold on to it. This was called "riding the blinds." Train robbers who wanted to board a train just as it was pulling away from the station would sometimes jump onto the blind and ride these until such times as they made their way to the locomotive and forced the engineer to stop the train.

BOILER
A closed vessel found on steam engines in which water was heated. A boiler was sometimes referred to as a steam generator.

COAL TENDER
A specialized rail car, located immediately behind the steam locomotive, that was used to carry coal, a water supply, and tools.

CONDUCTOR
The railroad conductor works aboard the train and coordinates the activities of train crews, oversees the loading and unloading of cargo, oversees

the safe and orderly transport of passengers, takes payment from passengers, and announces stations.

ENGINEER

The railroad employee responsible for operating the locomotive.

EXPRESS CARS

The train compartment designated an express car transported money, certificates, and other valuables. The first express cars were not designed to protect the contents from robbers since expectations for such were low at the beginning. For the most part the cars were made of wood, the doors and sides easily pierced by bullets. In addition, the doors were susceptible to being pried open with iron bars.

Oddly, the railroads and express companies were slow to respond to the threat of robbery, and more fortified express cars did not come about for twenty years. In time, some of the cars were fitted with doors plated with iron, but most believed such improvements were useless since any robber with a few sticks of dynamite could break into any car on the line. The railroad companies were also concerned with the expense associated with more bandit-resistant cars. It was pointed out to them that the rates associated with transporting items via express cars did not warrant the expense of bulletproofing and other improvements.

In addition to armoring and fortifying express cars, other modifications were made. Some of the cars had slits cut in the side into which could be inserted rifles to be used in defending against bandits. Some cars were equipped with Gatling guns, lanterns, and searchlights. Some cars were fitted with a steel cubicle at one end from which the messenger could theoretically hold off robbers with a rifle should the bandits gain access to the car.

One interesting, and effective, development came in the form of a specially designed hole in the floor of the express car into which an "iron cone" was inserted. While the robbers were milling about outside the car, the messenger could insert a shotgun into the cone. The cone would deflect the pellets, causing them to be scattered laterally. Any bandits standing nearby could have their lower legs sprayed with buckshot.

In 1892, the Wells, Fargo & Company introduced a "reinforced" express car. While it proved to be slightly more resistant to robbers, it could, in fact, be breached easily with dynamite, which occurred on occasion. Dynamite, in fact, destroyed numerous express cars over the years

EXPRESS COMPANIES

As the railroads proliferated the United States, it became clear to a number of businessmen, as well as government agencies, that trains represented a new and vastly improved manner in which to transport goods and cash. They were considerably more efficient and effective than stagecoaches, which had been the primary mode of moving such commodities.

The express companies leased cars or car spaces from the railroads. Two of the first entrepreneurs to determine the value and utility in transporting goods and money via the railroads, and subsequently formalizing such, were brothers B. D. and L. B. Earle. Around 1835, the brothers formed Earle's Express Service, believed to be the first express service to use the railroads.

On the heels of the Earle brothers came William F. Harndon, who advanced the use and reputations of the express cars as an efficient way of transporting drafts, notes, bills, and packages; precious metals such as gold and silver; and other kinds of goods. Harndon, a former train conductor and ticket agent, was familiar with the operations of the railroads and was well connected in the business. He also saw the value in advertising and ran ads in the Boston newspapers touting his business and stating he would "run a car from Boston to New York [and back] four times a week." In a short time, he had all the trade he could handle, and the express business was well under way. Before long, almost every train had an express car. If business was good, some trains accommodated two.

As the railroads expanded, so did the real and perceived need for express companies and express cars. Railroads around the country lost no time entering into extended business agreements with express companies.

In 1839 the Adams Express Company (AEC) was established by Alvin Adams. In 1845 the company signed a contract with the New York & New Haven Railroad, paying $1,000 per car pulled by the trains, an amount deemed rather exorbitant at the time. Rapid growth followed, however, and the AEC soon had hundreds of employees, most of them working twelve hours per day. By the end of the 1850s, the AEC handled most of the express business along the eastern seaboard.

As train robberies began to occur with greater frequency, the AEC hired armed guards to accompany shipments, along with detectives to assist in determining who was responsible for the theft of merchandise and money. It was the first company to do so. One of their first contracts was with Allan Pinkerton, who went on to found the Pinkerton Detective Agency. Some of the first men apprehended for theft of money and merchandise turned out to be AEC employees.

In 1850 the AEC was expanded to Buffalo, New York, to handle shipments for the Hudson River Railroad. Not long after, the company secured additional contracts with other major railroad companies throughout the East and Midwest. The AEC also handled shipments of money and goods via steamboats, which plied up and down the East Coast via a network of inland canals and into the Great Lakes. By 1858 the AEC was covering most of the midwestern states and transporting over $2 million per day. By 1862 the AEC had nearly nine hundred offices in ten states and had over fifteen hundred employees.

In 1867 the Merchant Union Express Company was formed in New York City and served to offer serious competition to the AEC. The two companies eventually merged into the American Merchants Union Express Company. By 1882 it had been renamed the American Express Company. By the 1890s the company was issuing American Express Traveler Cheques.

As the potential for Civil War loomed over the nation during the late 1850s, concern was expressed that all northern businesses operating in the American South would be confiscated. Anticipating this, Henry B. Plant, who was in charge of the southern division of the Adams Express Company, suggested it be sold to him. Plant implied that if the southern division were not sold to him, he would simply start a company of his own and take over all the AEC routes. An agreement was reached, and the Southern Express Company was formed. It soon took over all the express business related to Alabama, Arkansas, North and South

Carolina, Georgia, Florida, Louisiana, Mississippi, Tennessee, Texas, and Virginia.

Following the war, the Southern Express Company fell on hard times as a result of the deteriorated economic conditions throughout much of the South.

In 1852 Wells, Fargo and Company organized to take advantage of the growing express business in California, which was experiencing a mining boom at the time. A number of the founders of the company had previously been associated with the American Express Company. Not only was the company involved with shipping freight coast to coast, but it also engaged in the purchase and sale of gold. It was not long before Wells, Fargo became a major player in the freighting business with mail contracts and stagecoach lines. Eventually, most of their business was with the railroads. The company aligned itself primarily with the Central Pacific and Southern Pacific Railroads. By 1880 Wells, Fargo had 2,830 agencies spread across the country. It was also the only transport company that could move goods into and out of California. Between 1855 and 1917 Wells, Fargo was regarded as the preeminent express company in the American West.

As a result of this success, Wells, Fargo's money- and goods-laden cars became targets for enterprising train robbers with which the company was forced to deal for nearly half a century.

EXPRESS COMPANY SAFES

Attention was not limited to strengthening express cars in the hope of discouraging robbers. During the 1890s, the express companies applied some effort to developing safes to be more difficult and time-consuming to open. Since it was in the best interest of the train robber to conduct the heist quickly and efficiently, a near-impenetrable safe could prove to be a disruption to the process. In time, safes were developed that proved to be nearly dynamite-proof, but they were expensive. Some railroad companies opted not to purchase these high-priced safes, often to their regret.

The development of armored railroad cars and so-called dynamite-proof safes proved not as effective in discouraging robberies as the railroad and express companies initially believed they would be.

Robberies declined noticeably only when it became common knowledge that the express companies were transporting less money on the rails. It became less expensive and more efficient to ship money and other valuables by registered mail.

EXPRESS MESSENGERS

Express cars were generally accompanied by at least one messenger. The term "messenger" as applied by the railroads meant "courier." The messenger traveled in the express car, maintained the paperwork associated with what was being transported, and was, to a large degree, responsible for everything in the car. That is why most messengers were so resistant to intrusion from robbers, often refusing to open the express car door even under threat of death. Messengers often lost their jobs as a result of their car being robbed.

FIREBOX

With steam-powered locomotives, the firebox was a chamber that accommodated coal and sometimes wood to provide heat sufficient to create steam once the hot gases from the firebox were carried into the adjacent boiler via tubes or flues.

FIREMAN

The railroad fireman was a member of the train crew who shoveled coal into the furnace and tended the boiler on steam locomotives. His job was to make certain the train had the power necessary to negotiate hills and turns.

MAIL CARS

Mail cars were similar to but separate from express cars. Contracts related to transporting the US mail were also similar to but entirely separate from express deliveries.

Because of the increasing number of mail car robberies, the US Postal Service decided to do something. At first, the USPS determined it would be a good idea to procure armored cars for their railway operations, but in the end opted to strengthen existing cars. After the 1924 robbery of a Chicago, Milwaukee & St. Paul train at Rondout, Illinois, in which an estimated $3 million was taken, the USPS ordered bullet- and gas-proof armored cars. (In the Rondout robbery, the mail clerks were temporarily blinded and rendered helpless from the fumes of formaldehyde that was thrown through the windows.) This new postal car also boasted bullet-proof windows, slits in the sides through which rifles could be fired at bandits, and two specially designed holes through which flares could be fired during nighttime robberies to illuminate the area.

PINKERTON NATIONAL DETECTIVE AGENCY

Founded in 1855 by Allan Pinkerton, the agency worked closely with midwestern railroads. Pinkerton duties included investigating theft of property as well as dealing with labor problems and customer complaints. Because the Pinkertons were not affiliated with the US government, they were not subject to federal rules and regulations. The agency was often criticized for unorthodox methods related to pursuing and capturing train robbers, but in the end the railroad companies were satisfied with their efforts. Real and potential train robbers had reason to be apprehensive of the persistent Pinkertons.

RAILROAD POLICE

Impressed with the effectiveness of the Pinkerton National Detective Agency, by the 1870s a number of railroads decided to establish their own police and security forces. While express messengers and postal and baggage clerks were responsible for the contents of their respective cars, the railroad police provided a modicum of security. More often than not, they were involved with tracking down and apprehending the robbers. Members of the railroad police were referred to as "detectives."

Railroad police were generally armed with a handgun and a club, and were issued a badge from the company. However, few of them had any formal training as detectives, or for that matter, in any kind of police procedure. Their methods were often bullying and brutal. The railroad police, also called "bulls" by the hobos who rode the trains, were looked down upon by legitimate law enforcement officers.

TRESTLE

A trestle referred to a style of bridge over a gully, river, or any other type of gorge for roads or railroads consisting of a braced framework of wood or metal.

SELECTED REFERENCES

BOOKS

Betenson, Lula Parker. *Butch Cassidy, My Brother*. Provo, Utah: Brigham Young University Press. 1975.

Block, Eugene B. *Great Train Robberies of the West*. New York, New York: Coward-McCann, Inc. 1959.

Boley, Edwin J. *The Masked Halters*. Seymour, Indiana: Graessle-Mercer Co. 1977.

Breihan, Carl. *Rube Burrow: King of the Train Robbers*. West Allis, Wisconsin: Leather Stocking Books. 1981.

Dillon, Richard. *Wells, Fargo Detective: A Biography of James B. Hume*. Reno, Nevada: University of Nevada Press. 1986.

Gard, Wayne. *Sam Bass*. Norman, Oklahoma: University of Oklahoma Press. 1960.

Glasscock, C. B. *Bandits and the Southern Pacific*. New York, New York: Frederick A. Stokes Company. 1929.

Horan, James D. *The Pinkertons*. New York, New York: Crown Publishers 1967.

Jameson, W. C. *The Last Train Robber: The Life and Times of Willis Newton*. Guilford, Connecticut: Rowman & Littlefield. 2020.

_____. *Rocky Mountain Train Robberies*. Guilford, Connecticut: Rowman & Littlefield. 2019.

_____. *Texas Train Robberies*. Guilford, Connecticut: Rowman & Littlefield. 2017.

_____. *Butch Cassidy: Beyond the Grave*. Boulder, Colorado: Taylor Trade Publishing. 2012.

Kelly, Charles. *The Outlaw Trail: History of Butch and His Wild Bunch*. New York, New York: Bonanza Books. 1959.

Kirby, Edward M. *The Rise and Fall of the Sundance Kid*. Iola, Wisconsin: Western Publications. 1983.

_____. *The Saga of Butch Cassidy and the Wild Bunch*. Palmer Lake, Colorado: Filter Press. 1977.

Morrell, Ed. *The Twenty-Fifth Man: The Strange Story of Ed Morrell, the Hero of Jack London's Star Rover*. London, England: Forgotten Books. 2018 reprint.

Morse, Frank P. *Cavalcade of the Rails*. New York, New York: E. P. Dutton & Company, Inc. 1940.

Patterson, Richard. *The Train Robbery Era*. Boulder, Colorado: Pruett Publishing Company. 1991.

Pointer, Larry. *In Search of Butch Cassidy*. Norman, Oklahoma: University of Oklahoma Press. 1977.

Preese, Harold. *The Dalton Gang: End of an Outlaw Era*. New York, New York: Hastings House. 1963.

Reno, John. *The Life of John Reno*. Seymour, Indiana: Self-published. 1897.

Steele, William A., Jr. *Jesse James Was His Name*. Columbia, Missouri: University of Missouri Press. 1966.

Volland, Robert F. *The Reno Gang of Seymour*. Ph. D. dissertation, Indiana University. 1948.

Warren, Opie L. *A Pardoned Lifer: Life of George Sontag, Former Member of the Notorious Evans-Sontag Gang Train Robbers*. Self-published. 1909.

Webb, Walter Prescott. *The Texas Rangers: A Century of Frontier Defense*. Austin, Texas: University of Texas Press. 1935.

MAGAZINE
Edwards, Harold L. "Chris Evans—The Ready Killer." *NOLA Quarterly*.

NEWSPAPERS
Billings Gazette. June 14, 1924.
Decatur Daily Review. June 30, 1924.
_____. June 12, 1924.
Floresville Chronicle Journal. March 21, 2005.
Murphysboro Daily Independent. June 14, 1924.
New York Times. October 24, 1896, December 25, 1896.
_____. June 19, 1887.
_____. October 10, 1878.
_____. December 9, 1874.
_____. February 14, 1874, March 23, 1874.
_____. July 23 and 26, August 8, 1873.
St. Louis Democrat. September 12, 1873.
Waterloo Courier. August 27, 1924.
Wisconsin Rapids Daily Tribune. November 18, 1924.

ACKNOWLEDGMENTS

Whatever successes I have experienced as an author are due in large part to the inspiration, guidance, and assistance of others, including writers, readers, editors, agents, and publishers. For the past two decades, the most important of these was Laurie Jameson, whose vision, editorial expertise, and encouragement were responsible for the publication of my last fifty-six books. I miss her.

Thanks to my intrepid agent Sandra Bond, who works hard running the gauntlet of editors and publishers and who puts up with my inability to understand much of anything related to computers. She deserves a raise.

NOTES

CHAPTER 2
1. William A. Steele, Jr., *Jesse James Was His Name* (Columbia, Missouri: University of Missouri Press, 1966).
2. Ibid.
3. Ibid.
4. Ibid.
5. Ibid.

CHAPTER 3
1. W. C. Jameson, *Texas Train Robberies* (Guilford, Connecticut: Rowman & Littlefield, 2017).
2. Ibid.

CHAPTER 4
1. Richard Patterson, *The Train Robbery Era* (Boulder, Colorado: Pruett Publishing Company, 1991).
2. Ibid.

CHAPTER 5
1. Richard Patterson, *The Train Robbery Era* (Boulder, Colorado: Pruett Publishing Company, 1991).
2. Ibid.
3. Ibid.
4. Ibid.
5. Ibid.

CHAPTER 7
1. W. C. Jameson, *Texas Train Robberies* (Guilford, Connecticut: Rowman & Littlefield, 2017).

2. Charles Kelly, *The Outlaw Trail: History of Butch and His Wild Bunch* (New York, New York: Bonanza Books, 1959).
3. Ibid.
4. Ibid.
5. Ibid.
6. Ibid.

CHAPTER 8
1. W. C. Jameson, *Texas Train Robberies* (Guilford, Connecticut: Rowman & Littlefield, 2017).
2. Ibid.

CHAPTER 9
1. Richard Patterson, *The Train Robbery Era* (Boulder, Colorado: Pruett Publishing Company, 1991).

CHAPTER 11
1. Richard Patterson, *The Train Robbery Era* (Boulder, Colorado: Pruett Publishing Company, 1991).
2. Ibid.
3. Ibid.
4. Ibid.

CHAPTER 12
1. W. C. Jameson, *The Last Train Robber: The Life and Times of Willis Newton* (Guilford, Connecticut: Rowman & Littlefield, 2020).
2. Ibid.
3. Ibid.
4. Ibid.
5. Ibid.
6. Ibid.
7. Ibid.
8. Ibid.
9. Ibid.
10. Ibid.
11. Ibid.
12. Ibid.
13. Ibid.
14. Ibid.
15. Ibid.
16. Ibid.

17. Ibid.
18. Ibid.
19. Ibid.
20. Ibid.
21. Ibid.

ABOUT THE AUTHOR

W. C. Jameson is the author of more than 100 books and 1,500 articles. He has won numerous writing awards, including Indie Reader Book of the Year. Several of his books have been made into documentaries and as parts of past and ongoing television series on the History Channel, the American Heroes Channel, and others, and he was recently inducted into the Colorado Authors Hall of Fame. Jameson is also a singer/songwriter/performer and has recorded eight critically acclaimed CDs of original music. In 1999 he was named Songwriter of the Year by the Texas Folk Music Guild. He has contributed to the soundtracks for four feature films, two PBS documentaries, and one commercial short documentary. His music has been heard on NPR, and he wrote and performed in the musical, *Whatever Happened to the Outlaw, Jesse James?* Two songs written by Jameson have been included in America's Top 100 Western Songs list, and music videos featuring three of his songs have been produced.